COMING HOME YOUR WAY

Coming Home Your Way offers college and university students returning from an education-abroad experience a wealth of pertinent information, opportunities for meaningful reflection, and practical guidance on making the most of their time abroad. Grounded in research and addressing an array of aspects of education abroad—including intercultural communication, changing relationships, and career impact—*Coming Home Your Way* will be an invaluable tool for any student planning, experiencing, or returning from a stay abroad.

Drawing from theory and research from multiple disciplines, and real-world experiences of students who have studied abroad, the volume addresses key themes critical to understanding reentry, including individual differences in taking in experience, communication patterns and approaches, the reentry transition, the nature of relationships in reentry, bridging reentry and career, and more. Within each chapter are opportunities for self-reflection that allow readers to integrate the ideas presented into their own experience. Compelling short fictional accounts add flavor and detail that bring theory to life.

Coming Home Your Way provides a window into the complex experience of intercultural reentry. Reentry from an education-abroad experience can be a period of intense growth, and can feel disruptive and confusing while it's happening. The authors explain and explore these complexities in a conversational style that will engage students, and with the rigor expected by their instructors. Like no other book currently on the market, *Coming Home Your Way* will give college and university students insight into the challenges and intercultural opportunities that reentry offers.

Rick Malleus is a teacher and scholar whose work focuses on intercultural reentry. He holds a PhD specializing in intercultural communication, has published in the

US and Zimbabwe, and presented his work at regional and national conferences. He was an international student in the US.

Marina Micari has worked in higher education administration for fifteen years, and has published widely on student learning at the university level. She holds a master's degree in intercultural communication and a PhD in education. She studied in France as a college student.

COMING HOME YOUR WAY

Understanding University Student Intercultural Reentry

Rick Malleus and Marina Micari

LONDON AND NEW YORK

First published 2018
by Routledge
2 Park Square, Milton Park, Abingdon, Oxon OX14 4RN

and by Routledge
711 Third Avenue, New York, NY 10017

Routledge is an imprint of the Taylor & Francis Group, an informa business

© 2018 Rick Malleus and Marina Micari

The right of Rick Malleus and Marina Micari to be identified as authors of this work has been asserted by them in accordance with sections 77 and 78 of the Copyright, Designs and Patents Act 1988.

All rights reserved. No part of this book may be reprinted or reproduced or utilised in any form or by any electronic, mechanical, or other means, now known or hereafter invented, including photocopying and recording, or in any information storage or retrieval system, without permission in writing from the publishers.

Trademark notice: Product or corporate names may be trademarks or registered trademarks, and are used only for identification and explanation without intent to infringe.

British Library Cataloguing-in-Publication Data
A catalogue record for this book is available from the British Library

Library of Congress Cataloging-in-Publication Data
Names: Malleus, Rick, 1968– author. | Micari, Marina, author.
Title: Coming home your way : understanding university student intercultural reentry / Rick Malleus and Marina Micari.
Description: Abingdon, Oxon ; New York, NY : Routledge, 2018. | Includes bibliographical references and index.
Identifiers: LCCN 2018010975 | ISBN 9781138081758 (hbk) | ISBN 9781138081765 (pbk) | ISBN 9781315112749 (ebk)
Subjects: LCSH: Foreign study. | International education–Social aspects. | College students. | Intercultural communication.
Classification: LCC LB2375 .M35 2018 | DDC 370.116–dc23
LC record available at https://lccn.loc.gov/2018010975

ISBN: 978-1-138-08175-8 (hbk)
ISBN: 978-1-138-08176-5 (pbk)
ISBN: 978-1-315-11274-9 (ebk)

Typeset in Bembo
by Out of House Publishing
Printed and bound by CPI Group (UK) Ltd, Croydon, CR0 4YY

"Rick Malleus and Marina Micari know the scholarly literature on intercultural reentry, but—perhaps more importantly—they know the reentry experience personally, emotionally, and kinesthetically. Their wellspring of scholarship and lived experiences provides students with useful tools to understand their own reentry encounters. This is a small book with very big, and very important, ideas. It is about an area of intercultural communication that is largely overlooked. After an international sojourn, reentry into one's 'home' culture initiates changes that can range from the very positive to the very negative, from the transformational to the disconfirming. Drs. Malleus and Micari provide returning students with an approach to understanding their intercultural experiences that will help them to learn and to grow from their reentry encounters. It is a much-needed addition to the intercultural communication literature."

- Myron W. (Ron) Lustig, Professor of Communication,
San Diego State University, California, US

"In an engaging and thought-provoking style, the authors illuminate and unpack the often-challenging experience of students' return back into their own culture after an overseas study experience. By skillfully combining real-life examples and current interdisciplinary theory and research, they present tools and strategies for maximizing the insights and skills acquired during the overseas experience—and provide useful suggestions for marketing these new skills to future employers."

- Judith Martin, Professor Emerita of Intercultural Communication,
Arizona State University, US

"Malleus and Micari's new book provides a unique and welcomed addition to the literature on student reentry. Specifically addressing the returning student, the book skillfully provides an accessible but comprehensive survey of the scholarly literature while guiding the student through reflective questions intended to deepen understanding while providing adaptation tools. The authors have seamlessly combined developmental psychology, intercultural communication, and reentry research to provide students with a wide-ranging perspective on their transition experiences. Every student returning home from an international experience should have this book in their carry-on luggage."

- Nan M. Sussman, Professor of Psychology, The College of
Staten Island, City University of New York, US

"Malleus and Micari offer an exceptionally thoughtful resource for study-abroad students. The book is well organized and profiles the real-life experiences of students who have endured reentry culture shock, which is an often misunderstood and overlooked phenomenon. *Coming Home Your Way: Understanding University Student Intercultural Reentry* should be required reading for those students planning to study abroad but is also an excellent resource for any intercultural communication course! Very well done!"

– Jim Neuliep, Professor of Communication and Media Studies, St Norbert's College, Wisconsin, US

CONTENTS

Introduction	1
1 Lost at home	5
2 Personalizing your experience	16
3 Taking in experience	27
4 Types of returnees	37
5 Transitions	45
6 Communicating in reentry	56
7 Redefining relationships	68
8 What's new with you?	83
9 A new view of home	96
10 An emerging global perspective	107

11 What's next?   116

Conclusion   128

Resources   *130*
Index   *135*

INTRODUCTION

On coming home from studying abroad, four different students had this to say:

> "It was weird being back in my busy routine, as if nothing had happened. Everyone else here was the same but I had all of these new experiences."
>
> "It is always a rough transition… the culture shock of returning to the States is always more intense than originally going abroad to Austria."
>
> "American food kicks ass. I was so glad to be back in this culture and this insane country."
>
> "Perhaps the most difficult thing was getting back into the groove with my friends. While things often felt natural one-on-one, hanging out in large groups could be difficult as I had missed out on two quarters' worth of jokes and memories."

Each experience of coming home after studying abroad is unique. You may very likely be able to identify with some of the sentiments expressed above, but might not be able to identify with them all. That's to be expected. Even though each person's reentry experience is unique, there are also some shared patterns and reactions to coming home again. In this book, we explore the student experience of coming home after having spent some time studying and living abroad. This book will give you structure for reflecting on a reentry experience, whether you are in the midst of your reentry experience, are about to go home from a study-abroad term, or are studying in an intercultural communication class.

In order to most fully understand your time abroad in the host culture and your experiences back home, and to realize the personal, academic, and professional benefits of studying abroad, you need to do some work. That work involves gaining information and perspective, sorting through emotions, and enacting behaviors.

2 Introduction

This book will help you do that work. Being able to effectively communicate what you experienced, what you gained and lost from studying abroad, and what you plan for the future are critical for your development in reentry. This book will help you grasp those elements of your experience, and provide ideas for articulating your thoughts, feelings, and actions clearly, to multiple audiences. Taking a holistic approach to education abroad as it relates to reentry, this book will provide you with tools and understanding to weave your experiences into your life in ways that you find satisfying and beneficial.

Returning from a meaningful experience abroad—or intercultural reentry—cannot be defined as simply "coming home." It involves a process of transition, which for many people marks the beginning of a new path in life. Reentry can be a period of intense growth—personal, professional, and intellectual—and might feel disruptive and confusing while it's happening, but it eventually brings rich rewards that remain with you throughout your life.

Intercultural reentry means different things for different people, and it has been defined in different ways. Here are a few examples:

> "Cross-cultural reentry is the transition from the foreign country back into one's home country."[1]
>
> Reverse culture shock is the "temporal psychological difficulties returnees experience in the initial stage of the adjustment process at home after having lived abroad for some time."[2]
>
> "Reverse culture shock is the process of readjusting, reacculturating, and reassimilating into one's own home culture after living in a different culture for a significant period of time."[3]
>
> "Reentry… is a deeply personal experience and a cultural one as well… simply because reentry can be frustrating, lonely, and generally unpleasant at times is not to say that it is a harmful experience or a negative one… frustration, loneliness, and unpleasantness are very often the precursors of insight and personal growth."[4]
>
> Reentry shock "may occur when the individual returns home and must readapt to the once taken-for-granted practices that can no longer be followed without question."[5]
>
> Reverse culture shock "may occur upon return to the home country… may cause… distress and confusion… the home culture is compared adversely to the admired aspects of the new culture."[6]

As you can see, reentry has multiple definitions, all with important ideas embedded in them for framing the experience. The idea that reentry is a transition, the idea that re-adaptation to culture takes place during reentry, the notion that there may be a shock phase to the experience, the notion of home… all these ideas and more help define reentry.

You can also see that people call reentry different things: reverse culture shock, cross-cultural reentry, and reentry shock being the most common labels for the experience. We will use the terms *intercultural reentry* or *reentry* as they capture more than the 'shock' part of the experience that some returnees feel, and because the reentry process is much more than simply the reverse of culture shock.

We define intercultural reentry broadly as *the process of adjusting to life at home, after a significant intercultural experience in a host culture different from the home culture*. Reentry includes the process of reflecting on and making sense of those intercultural interactions, and of incorporating those experiences into your life back home, your understanding of yourself, and what you envision for your future.

Throughout the book, in order to explore and explain reentry, we will seek to answer common questions that many returnees wrestle with on reentry:

- What is *home?*
- How can I find a sense of *home* now that I'm back?
- What did my overseas experience mean for *me?*
- How do my personality, personal history, talents, and interests affect the way I utilized my overseas experience and the way I will incorporate it into my life?
- What do my old relationships with friends and family mean to me now?
- How have *I* changed?
- Do I see my own culture in a different light now?
- How can I communicate my new experiences effectively in both my personal and professional lives?
- What's next? What will my experience mean for me in the future?

How do we help you answer those questions and more? We do a number of things to help you understand, reflect on, and effectively manage intercultural reentry. First, in each chapter we discuss concepts important to understanding reentry clearly. Second, we will describe shared student experiences in reentry using the voices of students who have gone before you. We will do this through a series of student quotes in each chapter, and by providing vignettes that illustrate various stages of reentry, and the challenges and opportunities that accompany each stage. Third, there are activities in each chapter that allow you to individualize your reflections about your experience abroad and at home. Finally, we provide enlightening examples of academic research to help you understand the multifaceted transition of intercultural reentry.

We believe that the challenges and opportunities reentry offers you will be clear to you at the end of this book. Take from this book what is most useful for you, and keep in mind that students in a reentry transition—people in any type of transition, for that matter—often gain insight into their own experiences when they hear them echoed in a description of somebody else's. Engage in the opportunities for exploration and reflection built into each chapter. It's not always easy, but reflection can help you process your experience and develop in ways that are important to you. And finally, remember that there is no "right" way to have an intercultural, or a reentry, experience. Yours is yours alone, and what you will make of it is entirely up to you.

Notes

1 Adler, N.J. (1981). *International Dimensions of Organizational Behavior*. Boston, MA: PWS-Kent Publishing. Quote p. 232.
2 Uehara, A. (1983). The nature of American student re-entry adjustment and perceptions of the sojourner experience. *International Journal of Intercultural Relations, 10*, 415–438. Quote p. 420.
3 Gaw, K.F. (2000). Reverse culture shock in students returning from overseas. *International Journal of Intercultural Relations, 24*, 83–104. Quote pp. 83–84.
4 Storti, C. (2003). *The Art of Coming Home*. Boston, MA: Intercultural Press. Quote pp. xx–xxi.
5 Lustig, M.W. & Koester, J. (2010). *Intercultural Competence: Interpersonal Communication Across Cultures*. Boston, MA: Allyn and Bacon. Quote pp. 319–320.
6 Jandt, F.E. (2013). *An Introduction to Intercultural Communication: Identities in a Global Community*. Los Angeles, CA: Sage. Quote p. 311.

1
LOST AT HOME

CHAPTER OVERVIEW

In this chapter, we explore the idea of home. Coming home from studying abroad provides students with an opportunity to consider what home means in a variety of ways. We'll define home, consider reactions to home, and reflect on the observer perspective many students develop in reentry. We will provide you with an opportunity to consider the implications of how you see home, now that you have returned from your intercultural experience.

Reentry fiction: The first day home

Planes were lined up in the sky waiting to land at O'Hare airport in Chicago. Farai was shocked at seeing this, and more than a little anxious as his plane came in to land. The wheels hit the runway, and he breathed a sigh of relief as the engines roared, reversing thrust to slow down the plane. He was in America! Zimbabwe seemed very far away.

Four years later in 2014, Farai could hardly contain his excitement as he caught sight of Harare International Airport through the high, white clouds. He grinned to himself as he recalled his first landing in Chicago, and he longed to feel his feet firmly planted on African soil again. He had completed his degree in computer science, and was happy to be home after being away for so long. He hoped that his whole family would be standing on the balcony at the airport, waving at him as he walked into the arrivals hall in the terminal building.

After what seemed like an age, the jet-way was connected to the plane, the door opened, and the passengers streamed out. Farai felt a thrill of anticipation pass through his body as he walked down the crowded jet-way and felt the heat of the

Zimbabwean sun in the tunnel-like passage. As he entered the dimly lit terminal building, he recognized his mother and father, standing next to his aunt and cousin on the balcony. They were all waving widely, whistling and ululating in welcome. He stopped, put down his hand luggage and waved back with both hands, catching glimpses of a brother, sister, and some cousins. He rushed forward, eager to clear immigration and customs and see his family again.

His heart felt full, and he urged the next suitcase on the luggage carousel to be his. He had been a little embarrassed at the immigration desk, when the immigration officer had greeted him in Shona, and his mumbled response in greeting had felt foreign and unfamiliar to him. He hadn't spoken Shona consistently in four years, except for the Skype calls home, and the day that he bumped into another Zimbabwean at a bar in New Orleans. He thought that he'd soon get the hang of speaking Shona again, and paid no more mind to it.

The next hour was a blur of handshakes, hugs, tears, and huge goofy grins on everyone's faces. His aunt had kindly brought the family in her pickup truck, so he, all ten of his family who'd made it to the airport, and his luggage were piled into the truck. Questions flew back and forth, with Farai having hardly answered before the next question had been asked.

"What's America really like?" asked his dad.

"What did you miss the most while you were there?" his aunt wanted to know.

"Is your girlfriend going to come to Zimbabwe?" questioned his cheeky younger brother.

"Did you bring us any presents?" his baby sister asked hopefully.

In between the questions, Farai looked out of the truck window at the city he had missed and longed to see again. It felt odd to be driving on the left side of the road and on a badly potholed road at that. Some of the vehicles looked old. After a few minutes, the truck got stuck behind a slow-moving bus that belched clouds of thick, black, smelly smoke. "That bus would never have passed the emissions test in Illinois!" he thought to himself, but did not say anything out loud.

They drove past women carrying babies in brightly colored towels strapped to their backs and parcels balanced on their heads, lines of school children in their uniforms walking to school, men of all shapes and sizes walking to work… He had forgotten how often people *walked* at home and not for exercise!

The truck pulled up in front of his house, and everyone clambered out, hauling his two huge, overstuffed suitcases behind. A small crowd of neighbors gathered when they saw the truck arrive, mostly women and small children, some of whom he did not recognize. He was outside for twenty minutes before he had greeted everyone and exchanged pleasantries. Some of the kids whom he did not recognize had been born while he was away, so he met them for the first time. Speaking Shona still felt a bit strange on his tongue, but it was coming back to him quickly. He felt relieved at this realization.

A neighbor and good friend of the family, Mrs. Dodzo, had prepared what she remembered as his favorite dish, huku ne dovi (chicken in peanut sauce). He thanked her for it, clapping his cupped hands in the traditional display of thanks and respect, glad that this gesture felt natural and not forced. His mouth watered as he carried the pot into the house, and he couldn't wait to eat it accompanied with a steaming pot of sadza.

Home at last, alone at last, Farai sat in the bedroom he'd be sharing with his brother and stared out the window. He had forgotten how close together the houses were in the high-density suburb of Harare where he lived. If it weren't for the curtains, he could have seen right into the Kadengas' house next door. His parents' house—his home—seemed smaller than he remembered. Farai felt uncomfortable, somehow disloyal, to realize that after being home for fewer than three hours, he'd noticed all the things *missing* in his parents' home—things he had grown used to in the apartment where he'd lived in America. The TV here was small and not a flat screen; they didn't have a DVD player; there was no microwave, no wi-fi Internet access…

"Wait a minute!" he thought, "What am I doing? I'm just glad to be home again."

REENTERING STUDENT QUOTES

- "I came back and tried to recapture my life, but it wasn't possible."
- "Everything at home was the same. I was the one who was different."
- "Finding something to talk about and trying not to mention my travels was very hard and draining. They all just seemed interested in their little section of the world."
- "It was good to be home but I knew I would miss my life in Brussels."
- "When you love life abroad and you come home, you have a hard time falling in love with home again, because you know what else is out there."

What is home?

Like Farai's experience in the story, and illustrated by the students quoted above, returning home after studying abroad can feel like a whirlwind, with the initial excitement at seeing familiar faces and places and comfort of being back where you think you belong. But it can also feel strange and uncomfortable. Being home may not feel the same as it did before you left to study abroad, nor might it be as you expected it to be when you thought about coming home. All these contradictions and mixed emotions are quite normal. They are also connected to the first idea that is useful to consider when trying to understand the reentry transition, and that is how we think about *home*.

To start, take a few minutes to reflect upon what home means to you. Write down a few ideas before you continue reading.

Before you left for your study-abroad experience, how would you have defined *home*?

Often, living abroad has an impact on the way that we perceive home, no matter what our conception of home is. Perhaps that has been your experience too?

How do you define *home* today, having returned from studying abroad?

Was coming up with definitions an easy task?

For many students returning from studying abroad, defining home becomes much more difficult than it had been before they left. Often, students will say that home is a *place*. They might have a picture of their parents' house in mind, they might have their apartment or dorm room in mind, they might think of a neighborhood, town, or state as home. What if a student feels like they've "left part of themselves" in another place, like the country where they studied for a time or in their host family's house? Then the "place" definition alone doesn't really work that well for that student anymore. Does it work for you, in whole or in part?

Other returning students might say that home is the *people* around them. They might picture their brothers and sisters, parents, cousins, aunts and uncles when giving this answer. They might be thinking of good friends or roommates, or perhaps a significant other. What if there is more than one set of people who give them that homey feeling? Or, what if they feel their friends and family are having trouble understanding the experience they've just gone through and it seems a close connection with them is missing at the moment? Then, their "people" definition of home might not work so well for them either. Does it work for you at the moment?

For many returning students, home is something less concrete than a place or certain people. They think of themselves as being home when they are *feeling* a certain way. You know, feeling comfortable, where you can be yourself, where you can let your guard down, and feel relaxed. What if a student can't seem to find those feelings in quite the same way as they could before they studied abroad? Have you been able to feel at home since reentry began? How you think about what home means to you may need to be adjusted and reexamined if the "feeling" definition by itself does not work for you anymore

A place, people, or a feeling: for most returnees, it's likely that home is a combination of all those things and more. The idea of home is something that we often take for granted and don't really think about until what we have always "known" becomes something unknown, unfamiliar, or uncomfortable to some extent.

We agree with Torelli and his colleagues, who point out that the idea of home has connotations that are geographic and psychological, and that home can be thought of as a person's cultural in-group. In much academic literature, home has traditionally been seen as a relatively static entity, with a fixed set of values and practices, a fixed geographic location, and a fixed set of bases of affiliation (like norms, beliefs, and traditions). More recently, however, home has come to be seen from a more dynamic perspective, that looks at *when* a culture will guide judgments and behaviors, incorporates the idea of salience (importance in context), considers factors that inhibit performing culture (like cultural cues being present or absent), and explores the idea of being able to switch cultural lenses from one cultural home to another based on situational cues.[1] We urge you to keep this dynamic perspective in mind when considering notions of home, and how those notions link your education-abroad and reentry experiences. Remember that home is a cultural space, and this cultural space is transformed in part by media, migration, and communication technology.[2]

Reactions to home

Feeling "lost at home" is one of the most common characteristics of reentry. You might have been homesick during your experience abroad, eager to return to familiar places, people, and ways of life—but now you may find it isn't all you'd thought it would be. Here you are, technically back "home," but still somehow feeling a sense of homesickness, longing for something left behind in the host culture.

Consider the following observations made by students returning home:

> "I was glad to be home, relieved to be back on familiar ground. But at the same time, there were things about French culture I wanted to keep, but couldn't. Like the long, relaxed meals. The free-flowing conversation. The sense that family and friends were more important than work. We just don't live that way…"

> "It was really good to come home, but really hard at the same time. I made some good friends over there, including someone I was dating, and I really don't know if or how or when I'll be able to go back. I feel torn between my life here and the people I left there."

> "I feel like I don't know where I belong anymore. Part of me felt so at home in Italy—I loved the people I met there, the way they lived. But I know I'm an American, and there were a lot of things about Italian culture that were hard for me to get used to. I think it will take a while for me to really feel settled in here again."

Each of these students expresses a sense of ambiguity and confusion about where they fit best. But it's not just confusion over which culture is preferred; students also wrestle with trying to integrate their "new selves" into an old place. After all, part of being "home" is knowing who you are in relation to the people and things around you. When students return from a semester or year in another culture, they may not be so sure anymore.

10 Lost at home

Consider the following differences many students say characterize their "before" and "after" conceptions of *home:*

Before intercultural experience	After intercultural experience
• Feeling settled, grounded at home	• Feeling of rootlessness, "floating"
• Not questioning where you fit in; taking your place for granted	• Constantly questioning whether you're in the right place
• General satisfaction with predominant lifestyle around you	• Dissatisfaction with lifestyle; longing for aspects of host-culture lifestyle
• Assumption that you would always live in your home town, region, or country	• Desire to live away from home town, region, or country, at least temporarily
• Not questioning who your friends are, with whom you want to spend time	• Feeling uncertain about with whom you want to spend time
• Feeling satisfied with the leisure activities you've always engaged in	• Wanting to spend your leisure time doing new things, often related to the host culture

When a student returns from studying abroad, it may be useful to consider whether any of these before and after views of home resonate, considering which views of home do or do not reflect their thinking or feeling, and asking themselves why this might be.

Some thoughtful reflection might provide you some perspective on how your study-abroad experience influenced your views of home and feelings about being back. Take another moment to re-read the "before" and "after" characterizations of home and consider if they apply to your experiences or not.

The "observer" perspective

When someone has lived in another culture, it's unlikely they'll ever see their home in quite the same way again. They now have another perspective, a new "lens" through which to view their home culture. Part of the new lens was gained by seeing their culture through the eyes of people in the host culture. Part of that new lens comes from making new observations and thinking more about their own ways of doing, thinking and being than they might have done before.

Students may now find that back home they notice things they'd never paid attention to before, and these things observed about home may not be noticed by friends and family members. Do you have a newly critical eye for some things back home, and a new appreciation for others?

Consider this example: imagine an American student from Seattle who studied abroad in Zimbabwe, spending time with a relatively poor host family in a rural village in Masvingo province. When back at home in the US, this student might notice how "wasteful" her American friends are as they throw away a half-eaten apple, or leave an unfinished can of soda on the kitchen counter, later pouring out the contents and mindlessly tossing the can into the recycling bin. Her time in Zimbabwe might have made her aware of how people in that rural village always finished all the food on their plates and used everything for other purposes, like saving an empty soda can to store used cooking oil. Or, imagine a student from Mexico City who studied in Minneapolis, and when back home in Mexico had a newfound appreciation for the closeness of his extended family that he did not appreciate before living without family in America.

These kinds of new criticisms and appreciations realized in reentry enrich your understanding of yourself, your culture, and the world around you. At the same time, they can also make you feel that you are somehow on the edges of your home culture, like an observer rather than a fully active participant in your home environment. Has this been true of your reentry experience?

This "observer" status can sometimes feel alienating, especially when students are with other people who don't share their new views on some parts of their life and who have not gone through the experience of studying abroad. Returnees feeling this way should try to keep the following ideas in mind in understanding this part of the reentry process:

- Returnees' feelings come from newly broadened perspectives on the home culture, from seeing things never "seen" before.
- Returnees can—and will—use those feelings of alienation to help define who they are in the future. They are learning a lot about themselves: what makes them feel satisfied, frustrated, where they find meaning in things. Eventually, returnees will be able to make better sense of their current experience and the sometimes troubling feelings it has brought.
- Returnees are not alone; the majority of students who study abroad have some initial difficulty finding their place again when they return home. Finding these people, and sharing their stories, and seeing what they can learn from each other will help bring about equilibrium.

A useful way to reflect on home when returning from an education-abroad experience is to try to look at your home culture as if it were a completely unknown culture.[3] Why might you try this thought exercise? Looking at home through this lens (that is not informed by your experience in the host culture) might provide you with new perspectives and ways of thinking about home. You might have been told that being curious, taking some risks, and asking questions was a good way to get to know your host culture. The same advice can be applied in reentry.

What does the research say?

Researchers have explored the experiences of students who have studied abroad and returned home again. Let's take a look at some of the more recent findings to illustrate, in specific groups of students, the ideas we have been talking about in this chapter.

In interviews with Taiwanese and Sri Lankan students who studied in Northern Ireland and then went home, researcher Rosalind Pritchard found that 50% of the Taiwanese students reported missing people from Northern Ireland when they got home. This is an example of how home was defined in part as *people* for those students, and in Taiwan, those people were no longer there as part of the students' lives, making reentry challenging.[4]

In the same study, students also reported missing parts of the environment (place as home). For example, students in reentry missed the fresh air and clean water of Northern Ireland, and as one student said, "I also missed the countryside and the space which I grew to like and enjoy".

As you'll remember, home can also be defined as a feeling, and students in different studies have reported the feeling of *freedom* being missing when they return home after studying abroad. This feeling of freedom that was missing at home was reported by students from Russia, Liberia, Germany, and Cyprus who studied in the US and England.[5] Students from Sri Lanka and Taiwan who studied in Northern Ireland also reported missing this feeling of freedom upon reentry.[6]

Research tells us that students tend to idealize their vision of home while studying abroad and that when they get back home, that vision may fall apart. For example, Victoria Christofi and Charles Thompson found that students studying in the UK and US had held idealized views of their home countries during their time away, only to realize afterwards that home was not quite as perfect as they'd imagined, leading to a sense of frustration and disappointment. Another researcher, Feilin Hsiao, explored the experience of music therapy students studying in the US, and reported that some of these students found the US professional environment ideal, and so were frustrated about what they felt they were missing out on when they returned home.[7]

Not all realizations about home found in reentry are negative of course. For example, Susan Jones and her colleagues found that American students reported a new attitude of thankfulness for the things they have at home after being in impoverished areas of the world. This awareness came about in part by students realizing the privileges they have in their lives at home as compared to the lives people led in the host cultures in which they were immersed.[8] Another example can be seen where it was found that Taiwanese students realized that they preferred the speed of Internet connections and the banking and postal systems back home above those found in Northern Ireland.[9]

From these research examples, you can see that students from a range of countries have similar reactions in reentry. This realization should provide returnees some comfort and reassurance, as once again, it should reinforce the idea that having these kinds of thoughts and feelings about home is a normal experience for many students going through intercultural reentry.

The first day home: Considering Farai's experience

Before we end this chapter, consider again Farai's story that you read earlier. Notice how Farai is both consciously and subconsciously dealing with reentry issues connected to coming home, already, on his first day back. He is happy and excited to see his family—people are one way he defines home. He notices how much smaller his home feels to him than it used to—the place that is home seems a bit different than it did before.

On his first day home Farai notices differences between Zimbabwe and America. Some of those differences are simply observations of things he has forgotten about Zimbabwe while he has been abroad, like how often people walk to get from place to place, not for exercise, but out of necessity. Other differences he notices are essentially criticisms of home, like the smoky, polluting bus that needed a higher standard of emission control, or the older technology in his parents' house. Noticing these and other differences between Zimbabwe and the US is not something that Farai most likely expected to be doing immediately on arriving home. Feeling somewhat uncomfortable speaking Shona, and taking some time to feel his fluency coming back in his first language, might also have been unexpected.

When students return home from studying abroad, it is important for them to think about the differences they notice between their home culture and their host culture. Taking some time to think of and then list some of these differences is a necessary step in gaining understanding about the reentry experience. In looking at the list of differences a student returning home could come up with, it would be instructive to consider how many of the things noticed are simply descriptors of difference, and how many are evaluations or judgments about difference. How balanced would that list be for you?

Remember Farai had a mix of observations on getting home, some of which were descriptive and some had elements of evaluation to them. There is nothing wrong with making judgments about whether you prefer things the way they are at home, or in your host culture. The important thing to remember is to recognize the differences, acknowledge making these comparisons, and realize that this is a normal process in intercultural reentry. If home is always suffering by comparison to the host culture, however, then you may need to consciously focus on some of the positive elements of home for a while to assist in your readjustment, providing yourself a more balanced view of home.

Do you think it made a difference in reentry that Farai was from Zimbabwe and the country he studied in was America? Did the fact that he spent four years away from home without returning for vacations have an impact on his reentry? The answer to those questions is yes, those things matter. Just like Farai, your home culture and host culture influenced your experience abroad and reentry. Just like Farai, how much time you spent away from home has some effect on reentry. In the next chapter, we'll look at how different characteristics have an impact on both student study-abroad experiences and transitions home.

Notes

1. Torelli, C.J., Ahluwalia, R., Cheng, S.Y.Y., Olson, N.J., & Stoner, J.L. (2017). Redefining home: How cultural distinctiveness affects the malleability of in-group boundaries and brand preferences. *Journal of Consumer Research, 44*, 44–61.
2. Villalobos-Romo, G. & Sekimoto, S. (2016). A view from the other side: Technology, media, and transnational families in Mexico-U.S. migration. In Sorrells, K. & Sekimoto, S. (Eds.), *Globalizing Intercultural Communication: A Reader* (pp. 65–76). Thousand Oaks, CA: Sage.
3. Young, G.E. (2014). Reentry: Supporting students in the final stage of study abroad. *New Directions for Student Services, 146*, 59–67.
4. Pritchard, R. (2011) Re-entry trauma: Asian re-integration after study in the west. *Journal of Studies in International Education, 15*(1), 93–111.
5. Christofi, V. & Thompson, C.L. (2007). You cannot go home again: A phenomenological investigation of returning to the sojourn country after studying abroad. *Journal of Counseling & Development, 85*, 53–63.
6. Pritchard (2011).
7. Hsiao, F. (2011). From the ideal to the real world: A phenomenological inquiry into sojourners' reentry adaptation. *Journal of Music Therapy, 48*(4), 420–439.
8. Jones, S.R., Rowan-Kenyon, H.T., Ireland, S.M-Y., Niehaus, E., & Skendall, K.C. (2012). The meaning students make as participants in short-term immersion programs. *Journal of College Student Development, 53*(2), 201–220.
9. Pritchard (2011).

FOOD FOR THOUGHT

1. Why is it important for a student returning home from studying abroad to think about what the idea of "home" means to them?
2. What reflections about being back home by Farai would you consider *descriptive comparisons* and what reflections would you consider *evaluations*? Explain the reasoning for your choices clearly.
3. What causes some returning students to feel like observers in their home culture? Be specific in explaining your answer.
4. Research indicates that students have both positive and negative experiences when going through the reentry process. Why is this idea important to keep in mind when trying to understand intercultural reentry?

Suggestions for further reading

Klinkenborg, V. (2012). The definition of home. *Smithsonian Magazine*, May. Accessed April 15, 2018 at www.smithsonianmag.com/science-nature/the-definition-of-home-60692392/.

Kusenbach, M. (2013). Place feelings and life stories in Florida mobile home communities. In M. Kusenbach & K.E. Paulsen (Eds.), *Home: International Perspectives on Culture, Identity, and Belonging* (pp. 199–224). Frankfurt: Peter Lang Publishing.

Martin, J.N. & Nakayama, T.K. (2010). *Intercultural Communication in Contexts*. Boston, MA: McGraw Hill. Read "Cultural identity and cultural space: Home" (pp. 288–289).

2
PERSONALIZING YOUR EXPERIENCE

> **CHAPTER OVERVIEW**
>
> *In this chapter, we explore the many factors that make reentry a unique experience. Coming home from studying abroad provides students with an opportunity to consider how personal factors like their country of origin, race, gender, intercultural experience, and readiness to come home have an impact on reentry. We'll explore these ideas and give you a chance to consider how various aspects of your own identity and experience may have influenced your experience in the host culture, and your transition home.*

Reentry fiction: Glad to be home

"I'll get that done and in your email inbox by Wednesday, Ms. Whitfield," Jonathan said, and then quietly closed her office door behind him. Jane Whitfield smiled and leaned back in her comfortably padded, black desk chair. Oxford was looking better to her than it had in a long time; in fact, her life in England seemed just right. As she scrolled down her computer screen looking at the company's latest sales figures, she thought for the thousandth time how glad she was to be home again. Colombia had not been at all what she'd expected.

Holding her briefcase in one hand and her school bag in the other, Jane hurried along the college pathway through the evening drizzle to her class. Working full time and studying part time for her MBA in international business was difficult, but at thirty, she had the necessary discipline to see it through. That was why she'd taken the three months off work—one month paid and two months as an unpaid leave of absence—to do the immersion course in Spanish in Colombia. Wanting both the language preparation and the international experience, she'd felt sure a year ago that she was making the right decision. As she hung her coat over the back of her chair, switched on her laptop, placed her books on the desk, and settled in for her two-hour class, she wondered if she had.

The lecturer was droning on, circling the answer to another student's question, and Jane's mind turned to her recent experience abroad. It wasn't that she'd absolutely hated it, but it had not lived up to her expectations, and there had been parts of the trip that she'd really rather not have experienced. Take Jonathan at work today: he'd simply listened to what she'd asked of him, and then agreed to do as she requested, promising to get the work done on time. In Colombia, she felt that she would not have been able to hold the same position, managing a mostly male staff, as she did in England. It had seemed quite a macho place, and Jane was not sure she'd worked out how to navigate that world effectively. Javier had always seemed to have to help her with any important dealings with Colombian officialdom. That irritated her. People commenting on her appearance, near strangers asking why she was single at her age, the way that many women seemed happy with their way of life there—all these things had so annoyed her. She returned to Oxford with far greater appreciation for the gender dynamic in the UK than she'd ever felt before.

While the class plodded to a close for the evening, she found her mind drifting a little and Jane thought about her time in Colombia. She was happy about the progress she'd made with her Spanish language proficiency in Colombia, and there had been other benefits. She'd been able to try all sorts of new and wonderful foods, like arepas and sancocho. She'd learned to dance the salsa and vallenato well. She had been introduced to incredible writers like García Márquez and Laura Restrepo. Jane knew also that Javier and Claudia, her host family, would always hold a special place in her heart. In fact, they were going to try and make it over for Christmas next year. She'd really enjoy being able to repay their generous hospitality. "I'd better learn to cook a few good old English dishes before Claudia gets here," Jane resolved. As well as being a great kindergarten teacher, Claudia was an excellent cook, and quite house-proud. Jane thought guiltily of the overflowing laundry basket in the bathroom, her unmade bed, and the almost-empty fridge in her not-so-spotless kitchen.

As she drove home through the misty night, steering with one hand, and wolfing down delicious, hot chips out of a greasy paper bag, Jane realized how much she valued all the freedoms life gave her here in England. Kicking off her shoes, she plopped down onto her couch, clicking on the TV to catch the headlines on the ten o'clock news. She was glad to be home, she thought to herself, and relieved to be back in an environment where she didn't feel she was expected to fit into a tightly prescribed role. She wanted all the choices—and the uncertainties that accompanied them—that life at home offered her.

> **REENTERING STUDENT QUOTES**
>
> ➤ "This was always my dream—to go live in another country for a year. Now I've actually done it."
> ➤ "I've always wanted to be able to speak another language, and now I can."
> ➤ "I've never been a 'go-with-the-flow' kind of person, and I wish I had been more that way when I was overseas. But I also learned from that, and I think that will help me make more of my experiences in the future."
> ➤ "How I did not want to leave. I cried. I fell in love, so leaving was that much harder."
> ➤ "I wish I were back there sometimes… it's weird hearing English all the time instead of French."

An individual experience

"So, how was it?" When students return home, this probably becomes an all-too-familiar question. Has it been for you? Family, friends, classmates, and professors—all well-meaning—politely inquire about your semester or year abroad, and you, like most returnees, figure they probably expect to hear something like, "It was great," or "I made so many good friends there" or "I just loved the culture, but it's good to be home." And maybe those things are true. But the real answer to the question "How was it?" must take into account the multitude of factors that made your experience uniquely your own. Was it your first time living away from friends and family? Then it was probably sometimes a lonely experience. Did you come back with near-native fluency in a foreign language? That probably helped make it a very fulfilling experience.

A student's own particular characteristics, and the characteristics of their experience, will have a dramatic effect on the way they experienced time abroad and will influence reentry back home. Consider, for example, the following factors.★

★Adapted from the work of Martin[1] and Storti[2]

- **Stage of life**: People who travel when they are older often have a well-established sense of identity and may not wrestle with questions of who they are or where they fit in. But younger people—people in their late teens or early twenties—often have a harder time with these issues. They are in the process of working out their values, questioning the values that came from their families, their friends, and their cultures. And all of this figuring out "who you are" is hard enough when living in one environment; moving to a different culture makes the process all the more complex. On the other hand, older students may be more fixed in their views of themselves and their cultures than younger students, hence less flexible or willing to adapt to very different circumstances.

- **Intercultural experience:** Students who have already spent time in other cultures often have an easier time adjusting to life back home. Why? Simply because they know what to expect: they're not as surprised as "first-timers" are by the range of emotions and often-conflicted experiences that come with reentry. Even knowing what to expect, however, each intercultural experience is unique, with factors such as place, time, and a student's own stage of development shaping it. So while reentry for an "intercultural veteran" may be less challenging overall, it can still pose difficulties, albeit more subtle than those faced by a novice.
- **Length of time away:** Generally, the longer a student is in the host culture, the more likely they are to develop a sense of belonging there, making the reentry experience more difficult. But that is not always the case. Intercultural study programs are designed in different ways, and each person's experience is unique. For example, the longer a student was away, the more time has passed without their being around at home, providing more opportunity for changes of all sorts to have happened at home. At the same time, somebody abroad for a month isn't necessarily having a more "lightweight" experience than somebody abroad for a year: depending on the intensity of the experience, even a relatively short stay can be a life-changing event.
- **Attachment to host culture:** While length of stay may be a good predictor of how attached a traveler becomes, many students form attachments in a short time, and others may have many valuable interactions but not form deep attachments, even through a lengthy stay. If, for example, a student made good friends in the host culture, if they became close to their host family, or if the culture felt like a good "fit" for their personality, they may have a harder time readjusting to life at home than would somebody who hadn't formed deep interpersonal and emotional attachments while abroad.
- **Level of involvement:** Were you more or less active than normal in the host culture? Did you participate in social activities, or prefer to take in the experience on your own? The extent of a student's involvement with others and with the society will have an impact on how they feel when they return home. For many students, having been very involved in the host culture makes leaving hard. Some students, though, say that while they had fun and felt quite engaged during their time abroad, they're glad to get back to the pace of their lives at home.
- **Demographic factors:** Factors such as gender, age, race, and national origin can all have an important effect on the reentry experience.
    - *Gender:* Values and beliefs about gender vary greatly among cultures. As a result, a student may have been surprised at the assumptions people in their host culture made about them based on their gender. Consider these examples:
        - A US female student who had studied in Mexico described feeling "closely watched" by her host mother, who didn't feel it was appropriate for a young woman to go out socializing alone.

- A male student who described himself as "definitely not the jock type" says he felt much more comfortable as a man in France, where he studied for a year, than he generally does in the US. In France, he felt, men were "allowed to be more sensitive."
- A female student in her early thirties who had spent time in Greece says that while she valued her experience immensely, she was glad to get away from the constant questions about why she was not yet married.

These examples help illustrate the kinds of cultural norms surrounding gender that can affect a student's experience abroad—and different people will respond to these norms in different ways. Perhaps more traditional gender roles make a student feel restricted. Or maybe it is liberating in a certain way to have gender roles clearly defined. Whatever a student's reaction to gender differences in the host culture, its effect will not disappear once they're home. Returnees may, for example, find that they are more sensitive to gender issues than before they left. Or maybe they're more aware of attitudes about gender roles in their culture.

- *Age:* If a student is older than the average college student, they will probably find that, in many ways, their impressions of studying abroad were different from those of their classmates. Older students have already had a number of transition experiences, so may understand and expect the different stages of adjustment, and this may make their reentry somewhat easier than it is for the others.
- *Race:* Depending on the country a student lived in during their time abroad, their race can have a smaller or greater impact on how they felt about their experience. For instance, an African American student who spent time in Scandinavia said he often had the sense people were staring at him. Students may also have found that racism takes different forms in different cultures: in some places, particularly where it's not considered to be a sensitive political issue, it may be relatively overt; in other places, it may be more subtle, but just as penetrating, if not more so.

For students who belong to the majority group in their home countries, intercultural study can provide the first experience as a minority. Consider the following report from a blond American student who studied in Japan:

> "I got there, and suddenly I couldn't fit in anymore. Everything about me was different: my hair, my skin, my size, my accent. It was hard not to be able to blend into the crowd. And it was hard knowing that as soon as people saw me they would make certain assumptions about what kind of person I must be."

- *Country of origin:* Students often find people in the host country react to them based, in part, on their country of origin. Because the US has such a prominent political and economic position worldwide, it's not at all difficult to find people in any country who have strong opinions about US policy and culture. For this reason, many US American students report having felt like "targets" for complaints about the US while abroad. Students from the UK, Canada, Australia, and other parts of the world may similarly have encountered people abroad who had preconceived notions or strong points of view about their home country. No matter where you are from, these reactions will most likely have an impact on your reentry process, in particular on the way you feel about your home country and your acceptance or criticism of it.

- **Difference between home and host cultures:** While it is impossible to talk precisely about a "degree" of difference among cultures, some cultures are overtly more different from each other than are others. A much lower standard of living than students are used to, accepted values or norms that stand in opposition to their own—these kinds of differences can have a serious impact on the reentry experience. Returnees in this situation can find themselves torn between an appreciation for what they have at home and a newly found "critical eye" on their culture. For instance, US students who travel to developing countries often report feeling overwhelmed and troubled—but at the same time relieved—by the wide availability of material goods in the United States. Similarly, students who travel to collectivist cultures—ones in which the good of the group is seen as more important than the rights of the individual—often feel both let down by the fierce individualism in the US and happy to regain some of the personal freedom they had left behind.
- **Readiness to return home:** Some students find they just weren't ready to leave at the end of their study-abroad sojourn. Maybe they had just begun to make some good friends. Maybe they felt their language skills were really beginning to improve. Or maybe they were just having a good time and didn't want it to end. On the other hand, maybe they'd had enough of being in a foreign culture, felt homesick, and couldn't wait for their return date. Often, students find they have mixed feelings, reflecting an inner struggle between wanting to retain the independence they had gained as an exchange student and wanting to return to the comfort, and the responsibilities, of being a college student back home. The degree to which you felt ready to leave will have an impact on how you approach reentry: Students who did *not* feel ready often have a much more difficult time readjusting to their "old lives."

Describe and reflect

Many of the factors listed above affect not only how a student felt during their intercultural experience, but also why they decided to go in the first place, what expectations they had of the experience, and what they will make of it afterwards. Examining these issues can help you learn more about who you are, and in turn help you make sense of your experience in the context of all the other parts of your life.

To begin, try answering the following questions as honestly as you can:

- What are some words or phrases you would use to characterize your experience?
- What were some of the factors that made your experience what it was?
- Why did you make the decision to go abroad when many of your peers didn't?
- What were you expecting out of the experience?
- Do you think those expectations were realistic? Why or why not?
- In what ways did you meet your goals? What were some of your accomplishments while abroad?
- What do you wish you had done differently during your stay?

Upon reflection, some answers to the questions posed above may surprise you. Did any of your answers surprise you? Why? Why not?

Many returnees probably haven't given these questions a lot of thought before. They may also find that they hadn't been fully aware of some of the accomplishments they made and some of the many factors that contributed to making their experience what it was. It's very common for returning students to have the feeling that they have left something "undone" or haven't accomplished enough. If you're feeling this way, stop and think about your responses to the questions above. They should help you begin to see your experience in a fuller and more realistic light.

What does the research say?

Research has shown that there are indeed multiple variables that impact a person's adjustment in the host culture and their readjustment at home upon reentry.[3] Intercultural researcher Betina Szkudlarek[4] reviewed over 150 articles, papers, and chapters on reentry. From that research literature she found the following characteristics had been identified as having some kind of impact on reentry: gender, age, personality, religion, marital status, socioeconomic status, prior intercultural experience, and prior experience with reentry. Clearly, these personal characteristics are vitally important to consider when reflecting on one's study-abroad and reentry experiences, and help explain some of what a student is thinking and feeling in reentry.

Szkudlarek also identified situational variables found in the literature to impact reentry: length of sojourn, cultural distance, time since return, contact with host country individuals, attitudes of home country individuals toward returnees, and housing conditions returnees face upon reentry. So, once again her review of the research supports the ideas we have been discussing in this chapter. Your reentry experience is influenced by a whole host of factors, many of which you may not have much control over.

According to researchers Kelsey Gray and Victor Savicki, cultural distance is a factor influencing students' intercultural reentry.[5] Cultural distance measures were based on comparing scores for students' home culture versus their host culture, using dimensions of cultural variation like individualism-collectivism and power distance. They conducted survey research on eighty-one students from the US who studied abroad in different countries in Africa, Asia, Australasia, Europe, and South America. They discovered that "for students in study abroad cultures that were quite distant from the U.S. culture (High), reentry difficulties were high regardless of the positiveness of the study abroad experience." In other words, when a culture visited by students for their education-abroad experience was very different from their home culture, students reported reentry difficulties, regardless of whether they perceived having a positive experience in the host culture.

The length of a student's time abroad impacts reentry, although it is vital to note that stays of different lengths impact different students differently. A student might have a life-changing education-abroad experience that lasted a month, and another might be away for a year and the experience might not have a great impact on the rest of their life. For example, Janis Fine and Krista McNamara studied graduate students from a US university who had a two-week sojourn in Rome for a course that focused on cultural context and instructional leadership.[6] Some of the students they studied reported that their intercultural sojourn in Rome had developed their "ability to delve deeply into social justice issues requiring them to challenge the status quo and traditional pattern of privilege, and encourage them toward becoming advocates of equity-oriented leadership." That realization is a marked change in some of the students' outlook toward social justice back home that they can put into practice in their educational leadership positions. Their realizations were reflected on in reentry and came from only a two-week sojourn in Italy. This is an example of how time in the host culture does not have to be long necessarily to have a big impact on students.

Similarly, H. Tyrone Black and David Duhon found that students from several different US universities, who had studied abroad in London, England for just a month, also experienced some important changes in reentry.[7] The students completed pre- and post-sojourn measures, with results showing enhanced cross-cultural tolerance and empathy, as well as self-confidence and independence. A third example of research demonstrating that changes can occur in students who go on short-term education-abroad experiences is reported by researcher Susan Mapp.[8] Students included in this study went on sojourns ranging from nine days to two weeks, and went from the US to Thailand, Ireland, Costa Rica, and Vietnam. The greatest change measured just as reentry began was in students' perceptions of emotional resilience (the ability to regulate emotions in new circumstances). In her research, Annie Nguyen[9] found that there was an upward trend in the measurement of the fifty-five students' intercultural competence after experiencing a short-term study-abroad sojourn. Further, she found that those increased measures of intercultural competence persisted even three months after those students returned.

A number of studies on the impact of an education-abroad focus on language skills. For instance, Jeff Watson and Richard Wolfel studied students who spent a semester abroad in one of fifteen different countries, where the most common languages spoken were either Arabic, Mandarin, Russian, French, German, Portuguese, or Spanish.[10] In tests done upon reentry (that were compared with tests done pre-departure), the researchers found correlations between students' foreign language abilities and the time they spent in conversations in that language while studying abroad, and also with their participation in cultural activities. This suggests that students' level of involvement in the host culture, particularly having conversations in host languages and taking part in cultural activities, helped those students improve their foreign language abilities.

Research has also been done on stereotype threats and a student's country of origin. For example, Susan Goldstein[11] examined the idea of stereotype threats to American students having study-abroad experiences in 2016 when the US presidential elections were underway. From the literature she reported stereotype threats as being when students might expect to be judged negatively based on stereotypes held in the host culture about their own group, and that they might consider that they would confirm these negative stereotypes in the perceptions of people in their host culture. She reported that some students who perceive themselves as easily identifiable as foreigners in their host cultures (in this case as Americans) also perceive themselves as being vulnerable to stereotype threats. This research suggests that a student's country of origin does have some impact on their experiences in the host culture, and this may be especially true when those in the host culture perceive students, rightly or wrongly, to be representative of negative stereotypes of their culture.

Glad to be home: Considering Jane's experience

Consider Jane's experience from the start of this chapter. She is English and went to Colombia primarily to study Spanish. There is a high degree of difference between English and Colombian cultures. Those differences would be an important factor in influencing both her time abroad and her reentry. You can see that Jane feels a new appreciation for some elements of English culture found in reentry, as she compared elements of home and host cultures.

Jane is female, and her experience of some of the machismo elements of Colombian culture did not sit right with her. From this we can see how a characteristic of Jane's identity, her gender, influenced her time abroad, and provided her with a comparative lens through which she can explore and explain her ideas about gender now that she is back home in England. Jane is thirty years old, and given her position at work where she is supervising other workers, you can infer that she is a bit older than most undergraduates and has different life experiences. Her age is a factor influencing her experiences at home and abroad.

Jane enjoyed certain elements of her time in Colombia, and as she is pleased with her improved Spanish language abilities, you might infer that she was somewhat involved in Colombian culture, speaking Spanish with host nationals, perhaps with her host family. At the same time, Jane was glad to be back home, back in her routine, back feeling more firmly in control of her own life. You can guess that she was ready to return home to England at the end of her Spanish immersion program, and that readiness to return has an impact on the kind of reentry she would experience. How we experience things plays a role in how our time abroad proceeds and how we manage reentry. In the next chapter, therefore, we consider the different approaches we take to learning and taking in experience.

Notes

1 Martin, J.N. (1993). The intercultural reentry of student sojourners: Recent contributions to theory, research and training. In R.M. Paige (Ed.), *Education for the Intercultural Experience* (pp. 301–328). Yarmouth, ME: Intercultural Press.
2 Storti, C. (2003). *The Art of Coming Home.* Yarmouth, ME: Intercultural Press.
3 Christofi, V. & Thompson, C.L. (2007). You cannot go home again: A phenomenological investigation of returning to the sojourn country after studying abroad. *Journal of Counseling & Development, 85,* 53–63.
4 Szkudlarek, B. (2010). Reentry: A review of the literature. *International Journal of Intercultural Relations, 34,* 1–21.
5 Gray, K.M. & Savicki, V. (2015). Study abroad reentry: Behavior, affect, and cultural distance. *Frontiers: The Interdisciplinary Journal of Study Abroad, 36,* 264–278. Quote p. 273.
6 Fine, J.B. & McNamara, K.W. (2011). Community redefined: School leaders moving from autonomy to global interdependence through short-term study abroad. *Frontiers: The Interdisciplinary Journal of Study Abroad, 21,* 254–274. Quote p. 267.
7 Black, T.H. & Duhon, D.L. (2006). Assessing the impact of business study abroad programs on cultural awareness and personal development. *Journal of Education for Business, 81*(3), 140–144.
8 Mapp, S. (2012). Effect of short-term study abroad programs on students' cultural adaptability. *Journal of Social Work Education, 48*(4), 727–737.
9 Nguyen, A. (2017). Intercultural competence in short-term study abroad. *Frontiers: The Interdisciplinary Journal of Study Abroad, 29*(2), 109–127.
10 Watson, J.R. & Wolfel, R. (2015). The intersection of language and culture in study abroad: Assessment and analysis of study abroad outcomes. *Frontiers: The Interdisciplinary Journal of Study Abroad, 25,* 57–72.
11 Goldstein, S.B. (2017). Stereotype threats in U.S. students abroad: Negotiating American identity in the age of Trump. *Frontiers: The Interdisciplinary Journal of Study Abroad, 29*(2), 94–108.

FOOD FOR THOUGHT

1. Which of the factors discussed in the chapter most influenced your experience abroad and therefore your reentry? Explain why you think these factors are important to consider.
2. Considering your country of origin (your home country), what were three to five views that people in your host culture held about your country and culture? Did those views have an impact on your intercultural sojourn? Why or why not?
3. What influence did the length of time you were studying abroad have on your adaptation to the host culture and your reentry?

Suggestions for further reading

Nguyen, A. (2017). Intercultural competence in short-term study abroad. *Frontiers: The Interdisciplinary Journal of Study Abroad, 29*(2), 109–127.

Szkudlarek, B. (2010). Reentry: A review of the literature. *International Journal of Intercultural Relations, 34*, 1–21.

Watson, J.R. & Wolfel, R. (2015). The intersection of language and culture in study abroad: Assessment and analysis of study abroad outcomes. *Frontiers: The Interdisciplinary Journal of Study Abroad, 25*, 57–72.

3
TAKING IN EXPERIENCE

CHAPTER OVERVIEW

Our goal in this chapter is to help you think about how you "took in" your experience abroad, and what that means in terms of your life now and in the future. We'll ask you to reflect on aspects of your personality that may have influenced how you engaged with new situations in the host culture, and to consider how you made meaning from—and continue to make meaning from—your intercultural experience. We'll also take a more general look at how people learn through experience, and how you can continue to learn through your experience abroad.

Reentry fiction: Going with the flow

Andy remembered all the planning he had done before he left the UK to study in India. He had searched online to find blogs other students had written while studying abroad, and had read some posts that had really scared him, as well as ones that had left him excited. He had read three different travel books about India that a friend had given him. Andy recalled the fun and interesting conversation he had with Sonita, the Indian student he'd met at a gathering for international university students. Still, with all this preparation, plus the pre-departure orientation he had been through with his education-abroad program, he felt very nervous as he boarded the plane in London to start his journey to India.

Now back home, Andy was feeling some regret about the way he had spent a lot of his three-and-a-half months in Mumbai. He'd checked off most of the things from his "to-do" list that he'd created based on his careful research. He'd visited the majestic, breathtaking Taj Mahal in Agra. He'd dipped his toe into the Ganges river… Andy also had a "do-not-do" list that he had followed closely. He hadn't drunk any water out of a tap; bottled water only for the whole trip. He hadn't discussed religion with any Indian people he'd met…

Sitting at a table in the library café back in Manchester, Andy smiled to himself as he remembered meeting Seth, a long-haired, rather grubby, granola-munching American guy from California in his last month in Mumbai. Seth was outgoing and had struck up a conversation with Andy on a street corner. Seth had been in India studying abroad, but had taken a semester off from college to wander around the country on his own. Andy admired that quality in Seth. On hearing about Seth's stories, from his adventure riding a crowded bus through the Ramangara district on his way to Bangalore, to his meal with a poor family in Chennai, Andy realized that there were whole parts of Indian culture and different kinds of Indian people he had not yet met—or tried to meet.

For his last month in India, whenever he had free time, Andy went "off-list" and tried to "go with the flow" as Seth had. Andy had unplanned walks around Mumbai, ending up in neighborhoods and meeting people he never would have done if he'd stuck to his two lists of dos and don'ts. He remembered being scared, getting lost, trying new food, enjoying good conversations, meeting people from all walks of life… experiencing an India he had not imagined or planned for.

Back home, it was often this last month of his time in India that he thought about. More often than not, the stories Andy told his friends now were not about the Taj Mahal or other tourist sites he'd visited, but about what he'd come to think of as his more "authentic" last month away. He wished he had planned his time in Mumbai differently from day one.

REENTERING STUDENT QUOTES

- "Make friends with locals and practice speaking the language!"
- "I wish I had done more research on my country before going."
- "Independent travel—learning to be independent and accountable; sometimes it's good to have the experience of being lost in a different city where you may not know the language, i.e. when I went to France and got lost trying to get to the airport."
- "I didn't really understand the Catalans until I went to a protest. (Yeah, I know, against the rules, but SO worth it.) It really let me see how fierce they are and what a vibrant politically active culture looks like, and how that political activism is such an important part of their culture."

How do you take in experience?

If you think about the various people you know, you'll probably be able to identify a variety of ways different people take in new experiences. Some tend to try new things readily while others are more cautious; some enjoy engaging with many different people while others hang back, observe, and talk with just a few others; some jump in without looking while others plan carefully before making a move. These kinds of differences are well documented in research literature, and many have been shown to have an impact on individuals' education-abroad experiences.

Introversion and extraversion

You have probably heard about the difference between introversion and extraversion, which has been studied widely by psychologists and has recently received widespread attention in the popular press. In general, extraverts seek the company of many other people, and derive pleasure from active, stimulation-filled social situations. Introverts, by contrast, prefer smaller, or one-on-one, social situations, settings with less stimulation, and crave time alone.[1] It used to be assumed that extraversion was more strongly linked than introversion to desirable outcomes, but more recently scholars are pointing to many desirable outcomes of introversion. You can take an unscientific, informal test to see if you tend more toward extraversion or introversion using online tools.[2]

If you are more of an introvert, you probably found that during your experience abroad, you avoided large social events—like parties or big family gatherings. You may have sought out interactions with just a few individuals but spent time engaging in in-depth conversation with them. You may also have taken time alone to simply take in the surroundings, or reflect on the new experiences you were having. By contrast, if you are more of an extravert, you probably found yourself seeking out interactions with many different people, were drawn to very active environments, and engaged in activity most of the time. It is important to note that both of these approaches to taking in experience have benefits and drawbacks. Extraverts are more likely to have a greater sheer number of experiences within the education-abroad context than introverts have, and to engage with larger numbers of people, but they may not get to know individual people as well as an introvert would, and may not take the time to reflect on what they are experiencing to the degree an introvert would. In turn, an introvert would probably form deep connections and take time to just "be" in the environment, but may not have the variety of experiences or personal encounters that an extravert would.

Take a minute to consider your own tendency toward introversion or extraversion, and reflect on how this might have influenced your experience abroad:

> *Do you think you are more of an introvert, or an extravert?*
> *How did this impact the way you took in experience while you were abroad? What benefits did it bring you, and how may it have limited you to some extent?*
> *How could you play more on the strengths of your style when you are in new environments in the future? How might you temper your style to allow yourself to more fully experience a new environment?*

Comfort with ambiguity

Another personal factor that can impact an experience abroad is the degree to which people are comfortable with ambiguity, versus preferring to have a clear path ahead, or feel comfortable taking things as they come, versus preferring to plan and be able to predict more or less what they will encounter as they go through their days.[3] Again, there are benefits and drawbacks to each of these approaches. For example, the person who plans carefully is likely to have a smooth experience and not run into unforeseen obstacles; on the other hand, the person who jumps in without much of a plan may accidentally encounter a valuable experience that the "planner" might have missed.

As you did before, consider your own tendencies, and how they may have impacted your abroad experience:

> *While abroad, did you tend more toward planning and seeking to anticipate clearly what lay ahead, or were you more likely to take things as they came? How did this show up for you?*
>
> *How did those tendencies promote your getting the most out of your intercultural experience? How might they have gotten in the way?*
>
> *As you reflect on this, how do you think you might want to modify your behavior in the future, to get even more out of new experiences?*

Goal orientation

Like comfort with ambiguity, the degree to which a person focuses their energies on self-improvement goals versus goals directed at excellent performance can have an impact on their study-abroad experience. In a given situation, some people will tend to take a "mastery"-oriented approach to engaging with new material or experiences, meaning that they are focused on learning and developing their own knowledge and skills, even if that means they don't always perform well. Others will tend to take a more performance-oriented approach, meaning that they strive for excellent outcomes and are not primarily concerned with how much they are learning through the experience.

A large body of research[4] has illuminated the ways in which these approaches play out in educational settings. Generally speaking, people who take a more "mastery-centered," or learning-centered, approach to new endeavors tend to process new information with a critical eye, and try to integrate new information into their preexisting knowledge.[5] (There are more nuanced approaches described in the research literature, but we won't go into them here.) It is important to note that these approaches can change, and are influenced greatly by your learning environment.[6] You may even find that you take one approach in some settings, and the other in other settings.

Take a moment to think about the way you tried new tasks in your experience abroad—speaking a foreign language, adapting to new patterns of communication, learning the "rules" of engaging with a host family or friends. Chances are you were concerned with *both* "looking good" or doing what was expected *and* learning or improving your knowledge and skills. If you feel that more of your energy went into "looking good" than into learning and developing, you are like most people—you want to fit in and be perceived as competent. There is no shame in that! However, a focus on performance to the exclusion of learning can reduce your chances of growing through an experience. So if you feel that applies to you, you may want to try to focus more on what you can learn through an experience, and not worry so much about how you are coming off.

Experiential learning

The previous discussion relates to your individual approach to taking in experience. But there are also universal ways of thinking about learning. The *experiential learning cycle* model popularized by David Kolb,[7] and drawing on the work of psychologist Kurt Lewin and others, helps us understand the process behind effective learning over a period of time. The cycle has four parts.

First is "concrete experience," where we encounter a real situation—for example, a conversation with other students in a foreign language that you thought you could speak, but where you understand only half of what is said; or an encounter with a professor who seems angry at you, but you don't know why. Next is "reflective observation," where you take time to think about what happened, how it happened, and why it might have happened. You realize, for instance, that the other students were speaking very quickly and with a lot of jargon, or that perhaps there was some misunderstanding between you and your professor. The third stage is "abstract conceptualization," where you try to make sense of what happened by applying broader models to it. For example, you remember your language teacher saying that in order to understand fast speech, you'd need to keep practicing your listening skills, over and over. Or you go back to an article on cross-cultural differences you'd saved and realize that expectations about the level of formality between student and teacher in your host culture are very different from what you're used to, and that you may have inadvertently offended your professor with your level of informality. The fourth phase is "active experimentation," where you take into account what you've learned in steps 1–3, and make a plan for future action. For example, you might decide to commit an hour a day to listening comprehension exercises, and to ask more questions when you don't understand what somebody has said; or you might decide to read an article a week on cross-cultural communication differences in your host country, and re-approach your professor in a more deferential way.

Take a few minutes to think of a concrete experience that stands out for you during your time abroad. You can do this whether you were on a year-long program or a much shorter study or volunteer program. The experience should be something that was challenging for you in some way. Consider how you went through the learning cycle—and how you could go further in the future to deepen your learning:

> *What was the concrete experience? How was it challenging? Describe it in as much detail as you can.*

How, if at all, did you reflect on it at the time? What did you think about? Now, looking back, how can you reflect on it differently?

Were you able to make sense of it at the time in some larger way? Could you bring perspective to the experience that helped you understand it better? What new perspective can you bring now?

How, if at all, did your reflection on the experience change your subsequent behavior? Looking back on it now, how might you want to change the way you approach future, similar, situations?

What does the intercultural research say about taking in experience?

Researchers Melissa Steyn and Terri Grant point out that it is vital to consider what a "successful" return looks like, and to remember that the definition is not the same for all people or populations.[8] No matter the context of the abroad experience, different individuals set out different goals and have different hopes and expectations for their time learning abroad, and the realization (or not) of those goals, hopes, and expectations depends on a whole host of factors: your individual personality, the local environment, the degree and types of differences between your home culture and the new one, and so on.

Another important factor to consider is the challenge and difficulty that an education-abroad experience can present for a student. Intercultural scholar Geof Alred points out that the difficult parts of an education-abroad experience are easy to overlook, because people often want to focus on the positive.[9] It is also important to recognize that your experience abroad cannot be reduced to a rational set of logical choices, and that your feelings will have played a significant role in what you chose to do at every turn throughout your stay. As researcher Celia Roberts notes, "the experience of intercultural communication is an emotional one."[10] If you experienced some difficulty during your abroad experience—as many students do—such as homesickness, loneliness, or other difficult feelings, you probably were not always fully able to make the most of each experience. That is completely normal, and does not reflect poorly on your ability to learn or develop. In fact, navigating through a challenging experience abroad will have armed you with new insights and new resources to help you face future challenges.

Keeping all this complexity in mind, students need time for reflection. As is clear in the Kolb model above, using reflection to integrate your experiences into your life will allow you to identify benefits of your time abroad. This is a necessary (and often missing) component of cross-cultural reentry.[11] Intercultural development expert Michael Vande Berg and colleagues support this idea, finding that one element needed for successful study-abroad programs is time for reflection about the experience that is guided in some way.[12]

Researchers Lorraine Brown and Iain Graham, in a study of students in reentry, found that the act of reflecting on the experience abroad helped students better understand how they had developed interculturally, and how that development could influence them in the future. As the authors put it, "Reflection on the past year led students to confess to life-changing developments in philosophy and behaviour."[13] Scholar Tracy Williams concurs, arguing that providing returnees with multiple methods for engaging in reflection about their education-abroad experiences enables those with different learning approaches to consider and articulate what they gained from their sojourn. Carefully planned opportunities for reflection, Williams asserts, provide you with a way of "framing the experience in [your] own mind," thus better enabling you to use the experience productively.[14]

All this research should suggest to you as a returning student that reflection is a good thing! If you have not already done some systematic reflection (for example, writing, thinking about specific experiences, considering specific problems you experienced or are experiencing and seeking explanations for those problems), then make some time for it.

Maybe you wrote a blog while away, or kept a journal? Are there emails or Facebook posts you could go back and read that might shed light on what you were thinking and feeling when you were doing specific activities or having strong emotional reactions (positive or negative) while abroad? Use material like this—whatever you have access to—to help guide your reflective process. A good way to think of that material is as data, data that can help you draw some conclusions and find explanations for your current reentry challenges and opportunities. As adult-development scholar Sharan Merriam[15] has written, "For learning to occur, an experience needs to be discomforting, disquieting, or puzzling enough for us not to reject or ignore it, but to attend to it and reflect on it. It is then that learning takes place." In other words, it is not enough just to *have* an experience in order to learn from it. We need to pay attention to it and spend time thinking about it in order to gain the perspective, knowledge, and skills that can help us take fuller advantage of life's opportunities in the future.

In the intercultural context, this sort of reflection is somewhat similar to the ethnographic work—the participant-observation and writing about a cross-cultural experience—that anthropologists do in their investigations of culture. As Roberts writes, "The ethnographic experience helps [the student] to analyse and reflect on being 'in-between' and to think about the social, emotional and intellectual experience of being 'in transit'."[16] Roberts points out that the reflexivity inherent to ethnography—that is, the practice of raising your own awareness of and questioning your relationship to the new culture around you, and of identifying and critiquing the culturally based assumptions you carry into the situation—can help you develop a realistic understanding of the new culture, rather than an idealistic or overly negative one.

Going with the flow: Considering Andy's experience

There is no right or wrong way to take in experiences. We all have our preferences for learning and processing information. We all take in experiences in multiple ways, and taking in information during a study-abroad experience is no exception.

Andy, from our story that began this chapter, was a planner. He felt comfortable learning as much as he could about India before he went, and he felt that in order to be successful in his experience, he needed a plan. The plan Andy created included things to do and things not to do. Doing research on the place where you are going to study abroad is very sensible and interculturally responsible. However, as Andy discovered, his plan limited his experiences and thus limited what he was learning about India and Indian culture.

Seth, on the other hand, seemed to have no plan but to go where he wanted and to do what he wanted. This is not Andy's style, and trying to adopt Seth's approach simply would not work for Andy. But Andy was able to modify his own style somewhat in order to experience some of the things that Seth was experiencing. Andy came to see that unplanned experiences, experiences with some risk, paid off for him, enriched his learning, and made being in India more fun. In reentry, he regretted not being able to learn more about Indian culture and meet more Indian people because of his rather rigid plans. He still, however, had a rich, valuable experience in India, and his realization will help him have even richer experiences in the future.

In reentry, it is useful to think about how you experienced the host culture, how you learned about the people and customs. You may be considering whether you were a planner (an Andy) or a go-with-the-flow type (a Seth). Chances are, most students are really a mix. The important idea to take away is that we have preferences for learning and taking in experience, and those preferences influence how we interacted abroad and how we manage our reentry. Being aware of these preferences helps explain your experiences, but also gives you the power to step consciously from your preferred styles in reentry if you so choose. We'd encourage you to give it a try.

In addition to individual differences that influence a student's study-abroad and reentry experiences, the research suggests that there are different types of returnees. In the following chapter, we take on that idea, exploring the various approaches students take to returning home from an experience abroad, and giving you a chance to consider what your approach looks like and how you can make the most of it.

Notes

1 Hills, P. & Argyle, M. (2001). Happiness, introversion–extraversion and happy introverts. *Personality and Individual Differences, 30*(4), 595–608.
2 For example, see www.quietrev.com/the-introvert-test
3 Jackson, J.J., Wood, D., Bogg, T., Walton, K.E., Harms, P.D., & Roberts, B.W. (2010). What do conscientious people do? Development and validation of the Behavioral Indicators of Conscientiousness (BIC). *Journal of Research in Personality, 44*, 501–511; Chen, C.C. & Hooijberg, R. (2000). Ambiguity intolerance and support for valuing-diversity interventions. *Journal of Applied Social Psychology, 30*, 2392–2408.
4 See for example Elliot, A. (1999). Approach and avoidance motivation and achievement goals. *Educational Psychologist, 34*, 169–189; Elliot, A., McGregor, H., & Gable, S. (1999). Achievement goals, study strategies, and exam performance: A mediational analysis. *Journal of Educational Psychology, 91*, 549–563.

5 Elliot, A., McGregor, H., & Gable, S. (1999). Achievement goals, study strategies, and exam performance: A mediational analysis. *Journal of Educational Psychology, 91*(3), 549–563.
6 O'Keefe, P.A., Ben-Eliyahu, A., & Linnenbrink-Garcia, L. (2013). *Motivation and Emotion, 37*(1), 50–64.
7 Kolb, A.Y. & Kolb, D.A. (2009). Experiential learning theory: A dynamic, holistic approach to management learning, education and development. In S. Armstrong & C. Fukami (Eds.), *The SAGE Handbook of Management Learning, Education and Development* (pp. 42–68). Thousand Oaks, CA: Sage.
8 Steyn, M.E. & Grant, T. (2007). "A real bag of mixed emotions": Re-entry experiences of South African exiles. *International Journal of Intercultural Relations, 31*(3), 363–389.
9 Alred, G. (2003). Becoming a 'better stranger': A therapeutic perspective on intercultural experience and/as education. In G. Alred, M. Byram, & M. Fleming (Eds.), *Intercultural Experience and Education* (pp. 14–30). Clevedon, UK: Multilingual Matters.
10 Roberts, C. (2003). Ethnography and cultural practice: Ways of learning during residence abroad. In G. Alred, M. Byram, & M. Fleming (Eds.), *Intercultural Experience and Education* (pp. 114–130). Clevedon, UK: Multilingual Matters. Quote p. 121.
11 Braskamp, L.A., Braskamp, D.C., & Merrill, K.C. (2009). Assessing progress in global learning and development of students with education abroad experiences. *Frontiers: The Interdisciplinary Journal of Study Abroad, 18*, 101–118; also see Alred (2003).
12 Vande Berg, M., Connor-Linton, J., & Paige, R.M. (2009). Interventions for student learning abroad. *Frontiers: The Interdisciplinary Journal of Study Abroad, 18*, 1–75
13 Brown, L. & Graham, I. (2009, January). The discovery of the self through the academic sojourn. *Journal of the Society for Existential Analysis, 20*(1), 79–93. Quote pp. 82–83.
14 Williams, T.R. (2009). The reflective model of intercultural competency: A multidimensional, qualitative approach to study abroad assessment. *Frontiers: The Interdisciplinary Journal of Study Abroad, 18*, 289–306. Quote p. 304.
15 Merriam, S. (2005). How adult life transitions foster learning *and* development. *New Directions for Adult and Continuing Education, 108*, 3–14. Quote p. 8.
16 Roberts (2003). Quote p. 118.

FOOD FOR THOUGHT

1. What are some of the habits you had during your experience abroad that you'd like to modify, in order to gain more from future experiences? What are some approaches you can use to "practice" changing those habits?
2. Are there some situations in which you find yourself more open to new experiences, and others in which you feel more cautious? What are the differences between those situations, in terms of the environment, the other people involved, the stakes, your own confidence level, and so on? What can you take from the more "open" experiences into the ones that feel more challenging?
3. What can you take from this chapter into your current and future experiences—for example, school assignments, exams, job interviews, new job or internship experiences—to help you feel more prepared for some of those situations?

Suggestions for further reading

Cain, S. (2013). *Quiet: The Power of Introverts in a World That Can't Stop Talking.* New York: Broadway Paperbacks.

Nettle, D. (2007). *Personality: What Makes You the Way You Are.* New York: Oxford University Press.

Snivicki, M. (2005). Student goal orientation, motivation, and learning. IDEA Paper #41. Accessed May 13, 2018 at www.ideaedu.org/Portals/0/Uploads/Documents/IDEA%20Papers/IDEA%20Papers/Idea_Paper_41.pdf

4
TYPES OF RETURNEES

> **CHAPTER OVERVIEW**
>
> *In this chapter, we explore the different types of returnee styles. Thinking through these styles will provide you with an opportunity to consider what returnee style or styles apply best to you, what that suggests for how you are processing the reentry experience, and the implications for how you now view your home culture.*

Reentry fiction: Here we go again

"Brazilians are much friendlier than Americans," Tanisha stated with conviction. She had just returned to her apartment after riding the bus back from the university. No one seemed to want to chat with her on the bus, and this had really annoyed her. Her roommate Alice cringed, knowing that Tanisha was about to go off on another one of her tirades about the *wonderful* Brazilians and the *horrible* Americans. Alice was sick to death of hearing about how awful Americans were. Had Tanisha forgotten that they were both American? So, before Tanisha could get going, Alice paused the episode of *Orange is the New Black* she was watching on Netflix, shut her laptop and said that she had to study for a test the next day. She jumped off the couch, hurried off to her room, and closed the door.

Alice lay on her bed, pummeling the pillow to make a comfortable place for her head. It had been like this for two-and-a-half months now, and Alice did not know how much more of it she could stand. She had tried talking to Tanisha about how critical she seemed to be of everything since she'd come home, but Tanisha didn't want to hear about it.

The first few days of Tanisha being home in Wisconsin had been fun. Alice had scrolled through the hundreds of photos on her phone, admired Tanisha's new clothes, enjoyed tasting some of the new dishes that she'd learned to cook in Brazil, and had actually been fascinated by some of the stories that she had to tell about her five months away. Then, Alice had expected things to go back to "normal," but they hadn't. Tanisha wandered about the apartment speaking bits and pieces of Portuguese. She never wanted to go out to the movies or shopping at the mall—that was too commercial for her now! She sighed a lot, and when Alice asked her what was wrong, she'd say that Alice couldn't understand because she had never been to Brazil. Alice felt that Tanisha was acting like a sophisticated—snobbish—world traveler now. This, considering that before she went to Brazil, she'd never even been outside the US! She was also "all political" now, saying how the US exploited Brazilians… she'd never cared a bit about politics before Brazil.

Alice heard Tanisha clanging pots in the kitchen. "What exotic Brazilian dish was she whipping up now?" Alice mused sarcastically to herself. The other night Alice had suggested ordering pizza, but Tanisha had turned up her nose at that suggestion, saying that home-cooked food was the only way to dine, going on about the importance of eating together and taking time out to enjoy good food and real friends. It was only a pizza, for goodness' sake.

Alice understood that Tanisha missed her host family: it seemed that they had been very kind to her, and that she had formed a strong bond with the eldest daughter, Larissa. But Alice felt annoyed that Tanisha seemed to think her host family perfect, yet constantly found flaws with her *real* family here at home. Alice knew of the sacrifices that Mrs. Adams had made to save the money to send Tanisha to Brazil, but all that seemed forgotten now.

Alice heard Tanisha's footsteps coming down the hall and knew she was approaching her room. "Alice, do you want to take a study break and eat some of the quibebe I made?" Tanisha asked through the door. Alice felt guilty; she hadn't been studying at all and had been thinking not-so-kind thoughts about what she'd like to do to Tanisha. "Sure, I'll be out in a minute—thanks," Alice answered. As she opened her door, Alice heard the now-familiar strains of Tanisha's favorite Brazilian guitarist, André Abujamra, start up on her iTunes, and she smiled wearily to herself.

REENTERING STUDENT QUOTES

- "I fell in love with Korea and the people there, simple and sweet. However, I was happy about seeing my friends and family back home."
- "I learned to drive less, walk, bike, and take public transportation more."
- "I regret not being able to reflect more on my experience, but life has sadly seemed to move on."
- "And I've changed my plans for the future now that I've seen there is more variety the world has to offer that could still work with my academic career path."
- "…it was a little sad to go back to the usual routine of waking up and going to class."

What kind of a returnee are you?

While there are as many different kinds of returnees as there are people, returnees do tend to fall into different groupings: some bounce back easily, some have great difficulty readjusting, some make the intercultural experience a part of the rest of their lives... Consider the four statements that follow:

1. My intercultural travel was a good experience, but now I'm ready to get back to my regular life.
2. I really got to feel comfortable in my host culture, and now that I'm back home, I'm not sure how well I fit in anymore.
3. My intercultural experience has really made a difference in the direction of my life. I plan to continue on the path I started for myself while I was away.
4. I felt so at home in my host culture, and I *don't* have that feeling here anymore. There is just so much I don't like about my home culture anymore, and I'm going to try to make some changes in my environment.

Returnees will often be able to pick one of those statements that best describes their experience at a specific place in their intercultural reentry. Where do you fit in right now? Do any of the sentiments expressed above capture how you feel at this point in reentry, or how you might have felt earlier in the transition from host to home culture?

Intercultural scholar Nancy Adler[1][2] helps us understand some of the different ways returnees tend to respond to their experiences by categorizing returnees into four types. The following are descriptions of Adler's four categories below, which correspond to the four numbered statements above.

1. **Resocialized Returnees** do not try to fit their foreign experience into their at-home lives. They behave as if they had never been away, trying to get back into the swing of things as soon as possible. The overseas experience is thought of simply as an extended time away. While abroad, they tend to socialize mainly with others from their home country, and much less with host nationals.
2. **Alienated Returnees** are generally sojourners who have tried to assimilate to the host culture. When they come home, they long to be back in the host culture, feeling that it is superior to their own. They have trouble fitting in with old friends and colleagues, and they often feel unproductive in their daily lives. They know that they have developed during their trips, but they often do not know how to make use of new skills or knowledge now that they are back home.
3. **Proactive Returnees** feel optimistic and excited when they return home. They look forward to integrating the things they learned abroad into their at-home lives. They feel more productive after the trip than before, and they find themselves able to work with different kinds of people and ideas more effectively than before.

4. **Rebellious Returnees** feel they don't fit into their home cultures. They often actively set out to show disapproval of—and even make changes in—the home culture.

Adler suggests that there are two dimensions in considering how a person reenters their home culture (their mode of reentry). The first dimension she calls overall attitude, with polar ends at optimism and pessimism. The second dimension is specific attitude, with ends at activeness or passiveness. Each of the types of returnee discussed above falls into one subcategory from each dimension. So, a Rebellious Returnee's mode of reentry is generally pessimistic and active, while a Proactive Returnee's approach is generally optimistic and active. When considering Alienated Returnees, keep in mind that their mode of reentry is thought to be pessimistic and passive, while a Resocialized Returnee's mode in reentry is generally optimistic and passive.[3] [4]

Intercultural specialist Stella Ting Toomey[5] identifies three reentry types that we think are also worth your consideration here. She suggests that some people are Resocializers. These people tend to assimilate into their old home lives, and do not really appear to be different from the rest of their peers who did not spend time abroad. Alienators are people who do not really fit in back home; they claim to feel most alive and connected when they travel abroad, and might actively seek other international opportunities. The third type identified by Ting Toomey are the Transformers. These people tend to be change agents back home, with transformers tending to "apply multidimensional thinking, enriched emotional intelligence, and diverse angles to solve problems." Transformers don't really fear being labeled as different by those in their home cultures, and tend to be comfortable with changes in their identity. While Ting Toomey's reentry types were not specifically meant to describe only students, the ideas she discusses are clearly applicable to students in reentry, so we would encourage you to consider these three types as you proceed with your reentry experience.

Helping us to understand reentry further, based on her work in the field, Margaret Pusch[6] suggests there are other ways to categorize reentry styles. She proposes four categories: free spirited, detached, reassimilatory, and integratory.

You will see similarities to Adler's proposed style in Pusch's work. The *Free Spirit* reacts to the home culture with estrangement and rejection; this type of student wants to carry on their experience of being as different or unique as they were in the host culture (being foreign) and their behavior back home may be seen as eccentric. The *Detached* style feels a reluctance to simply go back to old patterns back home, but does not feel alienated from the home culture. This student type is concerned with creating a comfortable environment for him or herself, and is somewhat detached from home, but remains a tolerant participant in home life. The *Reassimilator* reentry style is happy to be back home, may downplay the international experience to those around them, may exaggerate home cultural norms for a while in reentry, and is cheerful with an easy intercultural reentry home. The final style is the *Integrator*. An integrating student blends the old and the new together, is pragmatic and fits into the home culture, but does not lose touch with their host experiences. An integrator continues to develop and change, and seems contented.

The usefulness of Pusch's work for you should be in seeing that there are a variety of styles in which students engage with reentry. No one style is "the best" and you need to decide for yourself which style describes you best at any given time upon reentry. Her work is also useful as it allows you to consider what style of returnee you are tending toward, and to consider the reasons for that preference.

We have seen that many returnees find that they deal with reentry in different ways at different times, depending on their moods and the people around them. So you shouldn't feel that you need to pigeonhole yourself into a single category. For instance, if you're feeling happy and productive, you may exhibit many of the characteristics of the "proactive returnee," and if you're feeling frustrated with the habits or attitudes of the people around you, you may feel more like a "rebellious returnee." Whatever the case, it is important to know that you are responding to reentry in a particular manner, a manner based on your unique combination of experiences, personality, and environment. It is important in reentry to be aware of how you are responding, and to then ask yourself why you are responding in that way. The answers will not only help you understand your process of transition; they will also help you make sense of your intercultural experience and what role you want it to play in your life.

Take a few minutes now to consider where you might fit along the dimensions and within the categories described above—again, without pigeonholing yourself, but taking into account the thoughts and feelings you tend to have now that you are home.

To what extent do you generally feel optimistic about the experiences you had overseas? In what ways?
Are there times you feel more pessimistic? About what?
Do you typically feel that you can make positive changes as a result of your abroad experience? If not, why not? What might stand in your way?

If you find that you are feeling negative or pessimistic about your experience abroad and return home, know that this is a common reaction. An intercultural experience can highlight for us what we don't value about our own culture, and returning home can idealize the other culture in our minds. Try to spend some time thinking about the things that you do value about your home culture, the things you're grateful for. At the same time, think about what action you could take to bring your own life a little more in line with the practices you valued in the other culture. Are there things you can start doing in your daily life that would make a difference? Volunteering you might do? Questions and problems you might study?

What does the research say?

Charles Thompson and Victoria Christofi[7] conducted research on students who had studied abroad in Australia, England, Greece, the US, and Zimbabwe, and then decided to go home to Cyprus after their studies and remain at home. A finding of their interview-based research was that two of Adler's returnee styles were most commonly experienced. Those styles were the resocialized and the proactive. They suggested that the resocialized returnees seemed to be using a coping style in reentry that reflected adjustment more than it reflected personal growth. In contrast, proactive returnees tended to focus less on adjustment problems, speaking more positively about Cyprus, and seeming to be happy to be home.

Researcher Tomoko Yoshida and colleagues[8] examined the reentry experience of Japanese sojourners. They categorized these returnees into *Bumpies* and *Smoothies* as returnee types. As the names suggest, Bumpies tended to report having difficulties readjusting to their home culture when compared to Smoothies, who in comparison reported less difficulties readjusting after their time abroad. One important way that the experience of Bumpies and Smoothies differed was that more Smoothies told the researchers that they had someone who accepted them for who they were post their sojourn. Bumpies tended to struggle more than Smoothies with issues around acceptance and identity. It was reported that more Bumpies than Smoothies perceived themselves to be facing discrimination back home because of their experiences in the host culture.

What we think you might take away from this research are a couple of things. First, no matter what reentry type/style you might be experiencing, having some form of social support, like a good friend or family member who can accept and welcome you home, is important for helping you manage your reentry. Second, the reentry style or types you experience may alert you to considering elements of your identity, important to you, that are being challenged or supported once you are back home again.

In addition to the specific reentry types discussed already in the chapter, we think that the work of Nan Sussman[9] who developed a model and conducted research (tested on American students who had studied abroad) is interesting information for you to consider at this point in the book. Sussman's research work suggests that upon reentry, returnees who have a weak cultural identity (feel the most estranged from their American identity) feel the most distressed. A further finding was that returnees tend to have lower stress in reentry if they perceive themselves to have an American cultural identity that is strong. It is important to realize the limitation of this study, with Sussman reminding us that the "current study neither measures nor categorizes sojourners into identity types. Nevertheless, the significant identity strength –repatriation distress relationship found here begins to hint at the identity types proposed." In other words, she is suggesting that there may be identity types that relate to the experience a returnee goes through when reentering their home culture.

Common to Stella Ting Toomey, Nancy Adler, and Margaret Pusch's work discussed in this chapter is the implication that some student types move toward attempting to integrate their education-abroad experience into their lives at home. Implied also is that some student types tend to isolate or segment their experience in the host culture, and do not attempt to integrate it into their lives in reentry. As intercultural specialist Bruce LaBrack suggests, "the pressures of job, family and friends, often combine to make returnees worried that somehow they will 'lose' the experience. Many fear that it will become compartmentalized like souvenirs or photos… and only occasionally taken out and looked at."[10] Clearly, whatever your reentry type at any particular moment in reentry, finding ways to *not* separate your experience in the host culture from your life back home is a good idea. As educators Vija Mendelson and James Citron[11] advise, in reentry students should "'unshoebox' (or unpack) their experience" as this allows some integration of the education-abroad experience into a student's home life. As we talked about earlier in the book, reflection is important in the reentry transition; as such, Adler, Sussman, Pusch, and Ting Toomey's work gives you another framework within which you may decide to guide your reflection.

Here we go again: Considering Tanisha's experience

Thinking back to the story that began this chapter, what type of returnee would you consider Tanisha? She went to Brazil, came home to the US, and seemed to be rather disdainful of everything American upon her return. Her roommate Alice seemed frustrated with the way Tanisha was behaving, finding her attitude toward America and American culture insufferable. Alice therefore wanted to avoid as much interaction with Tanisha as possible, not an ideal situation for roommates at the best of times, and certainly not ideal for Tanisha as she goes through the reentry transition.

You can infer from her behavior described in the story that Tanisha may be exhibiting the *Free Spirit* (Pusch) reentry style or the *Alienated* style (Adler). You could also guess that Tanisha may not really be fully aware of her behavior, and not really aware of how annoying her attitude toward American culture is, especially to her American roommate!

Alice is having trouble relating to some of Tanisha's changed ideas. For example, she is unused to Tanisha being politically aware, something she gained from her experience in Brazil. It is not uncommon, as you may find, for the family and friends of a student who has gone abroad to want that student to return to "normal" after a while back home. This may or may not happen depending on the style of returnee the student is. Most students are changed in some way, often profoundly, by their study abroad and reentry, and these changes are something we will explore in more detail later in the book. In the next chapter, however, we will consider the important notion of transitions.

Notes

1 Adler, N.J. (1991). *International Dimensions of Organizational Behavior.* Boston, MA: PWS-Kent Publishing.
2 Adler, N.J. (1981). Re-entry: Managing cross-cultural transitions. *Group & Organizational Studies, 6*(3), 341–356.
3 Adler (1991).
4 Adler (1981).

44 Types of returnees

5 Ting Toomey, S. (1999). *Communication Across Cultures*. New York: Guilford Press. Quote p. 250.
6 Pusch, M.D. (2008). Going home: Styles of reentry. In *After Study Abroad: A Toolkit for Returning Students* (p. 33). Brattleboro, Vermont: World Learning SIT Study Abroad.
7 Thompson, C.L. & Christofi, V. (2006). Can you go home again? A phenomenological investigation of Cypriot students returning home after studying abroad. *International Journal for the Advancement of Counseling, 28*(1), 21–39.
8 Yoshida, T., Matsumoto, D., Akashi, S., Akiyama, T., Furuiye, A., Ishii, C., & Moriyoshi, N. (2009). Contrasting experiences in Japanese returnee adjustment: Those who adjust easily and those who do not. *International Journal of Intercultural Relations, 33*, 265–276.
9 Sussman, N.M. (2002). Testing the cultural identity model of the cultural transition cycle: Sojourners return home. *International Journal of Intercultural Relations, 26*, 391–408. Quote p. 404;
10 Mendelson, V. & Citron, J.L. (2006). Bringing it home: Multifaceted support for returning education abroad students. *International Educator, 15*(3), 64–67. Quote p. 67.
11 Mendelson & Citron (2006). Quote p. 66.

FOOD FOR THOUGHT

1. What are the main differences between Adler and Pusch's returnee styles?
2. What advice would you give to a returnee who was exhibiting the characteristics of an alienated returnee? Support your contentions with clear rationale.
3. What is the utility of returnees trying to find which reentry style they might fit into?
4. Are there other reentry styles you would add to the list of those you read about in the chapter, based on your own experiences? Why?

Suggestions for further reading

Pusch, W.D. (2008). Going home: Styles of reentry. In *After Study Abroad: A Toolkit for Returning Students* (p. 33). Brattleboro, Vermont: World Learning SIT Study Abroad.

Sussman, N.M. (2002). Testing the cultural identity model of the cultural transition cycle: Sojourners return home. *International Journal of Intercultural Relations, 26*, 391–408.

Ting Toomey, S. (1999). *Communication across Cultures*. New York: Guilford Press. (Read Chapter 9.)

5
TRANSITIONS

> **CHAPTER OVERVIEW**
>
> *In this chapter, we explore the idea of transitions. You have already experienced a number of important transitions in your life, but the education-abroad and reentry experience transition is unique in many ways. We'll look at some models of life transitions and how the reentry experience fits into them. We'll also address some of the key challenges that people in the reentry transition face and how you can manage those challenges, and we'll consider how you can leverage your transition to explore your own academic, personal, and professional direction.*

Reentry fiction: In the hallway

Dana glanced at her watch again. "How long am I going to have to wait?" she wondered to herself as she sat in the hallway. She was not looking forward to talking to her academic advisor. Dr. Jenkins had no idea that she was about to drop her major in history, and she was worried about how he would react to her news. To him it would be like a bolt out of the blue, but to Dana, it was a decision that she had taken time coming to. It was her trip to study in China that had influenced her decision to change majors in the middle of her college career. She fidgeted, as the old wooden bench outside Jenkins' office was decidedly uncomfortable.

It had been a few months since she'd come home to Minneapolis from China. She had not wanted her experience there to end. Saying goodbye to all her friends, leaving her Chinese roommate behind who longed to come to the US but couldn't, missing the crowded bustling city—it had been hard for her to leave China. Her stomach growled reminding her that she'd skipped lunch. She also missed the food.

When she got back to the States, her apartment in Minneapolis didn't seem like home. Also, she and her old friend and roommate Nisha had been arguing lately. So, they'd agreed that Dana would move out at the end of the month. She didn't expect to see much of Nisha after that. Dana sighed heavily as she remembered that apartment hunting lay in store for her that weekend. She'd decided that it was time for her to try living alone for a while, so was going to look for studio apartments only.

She had felt relieved when she discovered a university program that let students design their own majors. After talking to an advisor in the program, she'd worked out a course schedule that would allow her to graduate on time, if she took a couple of summer courses. That would be a drag, but she'd rather do that then have to spend another whole semester at school. She would continue with her Chinese language studies, take some courses in the Asian Languages and Cultures department, and pursue a focus on intercultural communication.

Now, she just had to tell Jenkins this "good news." Dana remembered the first time she had met Dr. Jenkins. It had been at the department's orientation for first-year students. He had been the faculty leader of her orientation group. His enthusiasm for history had been a deciding factor in her asking him to be her advisor. Now she was dumping him—at least that's what it felt like to her.

Dana thought about all the students she would meet in her new program, and about the faculty she would have to take time getting to know. She knew most of the History faculty already and had some good friends who were history majors. She felt exhausted at the thought of doing all that meeting, greeting, and networking in the new program. But, it would all be worth the effort in the long run, she told herself. Wouldn't it?

The door to Dr. Jenkins' office opened, and a student she recognized, but whose name she had forgotten, walked out. Dana stood up, picked up her book bag and walked slowly to the door. She was about to end another chapter in her life, and was not sure if she was making the right decision. She had been so sure that history was what she wanted to study when she came to college. Last night she had been so sure that it was not. Now, as she smiled hesitantly at Dr. Jenkins and closed the office door, she felt like she wasn't quite sure of anything.

REENTERING STUDENT QUOTES

- "In the car from the airport, I started crying at seeing the wide roads and lawns that I hadn't seen in four months, and realized I was actually home again."
- "I make my bed and get up early nowadays. Just makes me feel more adult."
- "Coming home was very refreshing to me. Studying abroad gives you a lot of confidence and skills that I couldn't imagine possessing in any other way other than studying abroad."

> "I feel like I have a greater appreciation for simpler living, and I'm aware of how large our world truly is."

Endings and beginnings

Those who study life transitions agree that today, transition is "a fundamental feature of life."[1] For returnees, we believe this is even truer. After studying abroad, a student is experiencing reentry at the same time as another major transition in their life: going to college or university. The university period is often described as a time of great change and growth, or as scholars Jenna Stephenson-Abetz and Amanda Holman put it, "a transitional period of development typified by newfound freedom and independence, exposure to new ideas, new ways of thinking and diverse student populations."[2] In other words, the experience of being a college or university student is itself a major life change. Add to that going abroad to study, and then coming home again and integrating that experience into your home world again, and the already major transition is intensified. It's not surprising, then, that students in reentry need to have mechanisms in place to help them understand and manage the reentry transition. As advocates of lifelong learning Robert Ingram, John Field, and Jim Gallacher remind us, "each person must expect and make ready for transitions and engage in learning as a fundamental strategy for handling change."[3]

Reentry has been conceptualized as part of a complex transition cycle that connects home and host culture.[4] The following sentiments are ones we have heard many returnees express, and they may (or may not) be true for you:

- These days, I just don't feel a part of what's around me. I don't feel like I belong in the way I used to.
- I used to feel like I knew exactly who I was, what I valued and wanted to do, but now I'm not so sure anymore.
- I often feel disappointed in people and things now that I'm home, as if they just don't meet my expectations.
- Lately, I feel confused about my direction. I used to feel clearer about my place in life, but now I'm not sure where I am, or where I want to be.

Each of these statements illustrates one stage in the process of going through a transition, as described by William Bridges, author of *Transitions: Making Sense of Life's Changes*.[5] To view your intercultural experience realistically, understand that in many ways it is a transition much like any other. Graduating from school and starting a working life, ending a relationship and going off on your own, moving to a new city—these are all transitions, and they all have a lot in common with the transition of intercultural reentry.

Bridges identifies four stages people go through when they come to the end of an experience, like a relationship, a job, or an immersive intercultural experience.

First, he writes, we feel "disengaged," or separated from the world around us. Next, we feel a sense of "disidentification." This means not just that we feel less sure of who we are, but also of where we fit in. In the third stage, "disenchantment," we may feel sad or depressed, feeling discouraged that things are not what we had hoped for. Finally, we enter the "disorientation" stage: we feel confused, we're not quite sure where we are in our lives, and we're not sure where to head next. While they can be emotionally painful, Bridges notes, these stages are a necessary and helpful part of working through any kind of transition. Going through this process helps "free us up" to integrate those old experiences into new ones.

Lost in flux

When you think about the transition period in which you currently find yourself, try to articulate the best ways to describe how you are feeling. For instance, do any of these words ring true for you currently?

1. clear-headed	4. alienated	7. between things	10. constantly changing
2. confused	5. excited	8. anticipating	11. unsure
3. eager	6. in limbo	9. certain	12. comfortable

Are there other words you would add?

As you probably noticed, there are a couple of themes here. Numbers 2, 4, 6, 7, 10, and 11 suggest the feeling of being in an "empty space," not knowing exactly which direction to turn next, and many returnees may identify with those descriptors. However, many returnees may also feel much the opposite: glad to be home, excited about what lies ahead, and eager to put new skills and interests into practice. Numbers 1, 3, 5, 8, 9, and 12 suggest that theme. There is no right or wrong way to be feeling after an experience abroad. Different people move through transitions in different ways, and each education-abroad experience is unique—so it's really not worth comparing your reaction to anybody else's. Later in the chapter, we'll explore some of the factors that can influence an individual person's reaction to a reentry experience, and make yours unique.

Remember that while reentry is a special kind of transition, you have likely been through many transitions already in your life that may have been disruptive, exciting, unsettling, or rewarding. Those might include major milestone birthdays as a time of transition, or starting in a new school, or ending secondary school and starting university, parents divorcing or remarrying, or getting a driver's license and the newfound freedom and responsibility that brings.

As developmental psychologist Michael Basseches[6] wrote several decades ago, "Facing the tensions involved when an existing structure seems to be working less well, and facing the need for a new structure when one's previous structure has been dismantled, are likely to command much of individuals' attention on repeated occasions during their life-spans." Put plainly, there will inevitably be times of change in your life when the relationships you have had, the study or work you have been engaged in, the perspectives and assumptions you have held—whatever it may be—will no longer feel adequate. And managing the process of rethinking these facets of your life, and in some cases of reconstructing them, will take up a lot of your energy.

Bridges reminds us to recognize that moving from one phase of life to another is rarely easy, and that to help that process unfold, we can consider how we have managed ending one phase and entering another in the past—and how we might like to do that differently (or not) now. Try to recall the ways you have managed previous transitions in your life, the expectations you had that were or were not realized, the new benefits you gained after the transition, and the things you may have lost. In all likelihood, there are meaningful parallels you can draw between those experiences and your current reentry experience.

> *Think of one or two previous transitions you've experienced in your life. How would you describe those?*
>
> *What strategies did you use to manage those transitions? Which do you feel were successful strategies, and which less so? If you could do it over again, what might you do differently? What might you do the same?*
>
> *What lessons can you draw from your previous transitions to help you manage the reentry transition?*

Bridges advises that we accept our reactions to the loss of an old way of being (your "pre-departure self"), and that we intentionally reflect on our feelings about the transition. For instance, what about you is changing or has changed? What fundamental qualities are staying the same? What parts of the change are you glad about, and which, if any, do you have mixed feelings about? Bridges also reminds us that there will be a "neutral zone," a period of limbo where we don't feel solidly in one place or another. Maybe, for example, you've met a new group of friends who share your new international perspectives, but part of you longs to spend time with your old friends, even though being in conversations with them now can sometimes be frustrating. This kind of limbo can feel uncomfortable, and it's easy to wish it away. But it's part of the process. If this is where you find yourself, Bridges advises, try to keep connecting with others, stay engaged in what really interests you, and take time to envision and plan for new activities or projects in the future.

Regardless of what country you started from, and whether you were on a year-long sojourn or a two-week volunteer trip, the experience of changing your cultural environment and returning home is usually uncomfortable in some pretty significant ways—and that's part of the reason it can be such a meaningful learning experience. But remember that you don't need to do it alone: Support during the reentry process is important and can help ease the transition.[7] Because reentry is such a big transition, it's not uncommon for people to feel anxious or depressed during or after a significant experience abroad.[8] If you feel like you're having a lot of difficulty adjusting to life back home, or that you are simply not feeling good since your return, we encourage you to talk with a psychologist, social worker, or other counselor in your university's health service or in your community. If you don't feel like you're ready for that, start by talking with a trusted friend.

Take stock, too, of the beneficial aspects of the transition process. As long as the difficulty is not debilitating, facing and overcoming the challenge of a transition can bring important rewards—such as broadened perspectives, a stronger sense of who you are and want to be, and greater confidence in your ability to persevere. Transitions can be a time of creativity, of trying out new ideas and approaches, of great learning.[9] So, take care of yourself, but recognize that you are growing in the process.

Changing perspectives

Most of the time, education-abroad experiences lead to some kind of perspective change in the individual taking the journey. You have probably already noticed that you look at things from a slightly different angle now. Maybe you notice the size of homes, streets, or food portions in your home country as compared to your host country. Maybe you are more aware of the biases or assumptions of friends and family about foreign cultures than you used to be. Or maybe you see your *own* habits, assumptions, and preferences with a new critical eye. A number of scholars, including Jack Mezirow and Peter Jarvis,[10] have written about learning that is transformational—that changes you in some fundamental way. Often, an education-abroad experience leads to this kind of learning. Models of transformational learning typically start with some sort of rupture or disruption to the status quo, a "disorienting dilemma" (Mezirow) or a "disjuncture" (Jarvis). The idea here is that when meaningful learning—the kind of learning that changes you somehow as a person—occurs, it is triggered by an experience that challenges your assumptions, values, beliefs, or way of understanding the world around you. After such an event, you are likely to reflect on that event, and often you will decide to take some action to resolve the conflict you are feeling—and during this process you may feel accompanying confusion, frustration, or other emotion. At the end of the experience, you "re-enter" your life with some new perspective, which may be a modest shift or might be a radically new way of looking at yourself and the world. As Kathryn Ecclestone[11] has written, transition means not just moving to the next thing, but in some sense "unbecoming" what you were before.

Take a few minutes to think about how your perspectives may have changed as a result of your education-abroad experience.

> *What are some of the "triggering events" you experienced while abroad—situations that disrupted your comfort or assumptions?*
> *How did you react, both at the time and later upon reflection? What were your thoughts, feelings, and actions?*
> *How do you think your perspective may have changed as a result of these events? How about as a result of your whole experience abroad? (Remember, this does not need to be a radical shift in perspective.)*

Do you feel that you have been able to integrate your new perspectives into your life back at home? If not, what stands in the way, and how might you begin to move around that barrier?

In addition to new perspectives, a transition such as returning home can also bring a changed identity, and sense of agency—or a person's ability to shape their own path in interaction with others.[12] Another way of thinking about this, in Eccleston's words, is that transitions "combine turning points, milestones or life events with subtle, complex processes of 'becoming somebody' personally, educationally and occupationally" (pp. 12–13). You may have found yourself rethinking "who you are" in addition to working through considering how you may be able to shape your own life path from here forward.

Consider:

How is your sense of who you are different, if at all, now from before you left?
How, if at all, has your experience abroad helped you rethink who you want to become, personally, academically, or professionally?
How might your experience abroad have helped you better understand your agency—or your ability to forge a path forward for yourself?

What does the research say?

As we noted earlier, there is a good deal of evidence in the research that "repatriation," or coming back to your home country after a stay abroad, is a difficult process for many people, across a number of different kinds of overseas sojourns.[13] The extent to which a person will experience difficulty during the reentry transition depends on a number of factors, including their particular personality and skills, whether or not they have previously spent time overseas, the degree of difference between their home culture and the one they visited, and the amount of social support they have upon return.[14] Another key factor seems to be whether or not a person was prepared for the challenge of the transition. We all expect living abroad to be hard, but most people expect coming home to be easy. Not surprisingly, people who are prepared for the challenges of coming home tend to have an easier time readjusting to life back in their home countries.[15]

For example, in a study of New Zealand students returning home after a sojourn abroad, Joy Rogers and Colleen Ward found that those whose actual experiences abroad were more difficult than they had anticipated experienced high levels of psychological distress, as compared to other students whose expectations more closely matched their actual experience.[16] Keep in mind here that most people *are* unprepared for reentry, having focused most of their energy on gearing up for the abroad experience itself, and on living it while abroad—but not on what would happen after it had ended.

The degree to which a person begins to shed their home culture identity during and after an experience abroad has also been shown to affect the transition back home. For example, in a study by scholar Nan Sussman, American businesspeople who reported feeling "less American" after an overseas post also reported a more difficult transition back home than did those whose sense of "Americanness" was left intact.[17] Along the same lines, researcher Louise Kidder found that Japanese returnees experienced a sense of being "less Japanese" because of changes in their appearance, nonverbal behavior, or interpersonal style after having spent time abroad, and this caused discomfort—for some, so much so that they tried to hide their new "foreignness."[18]

This feeling of being less connected to one's home culture has implications for self-identity. In an ethnographic study of international students in the UK, researcher Lorraine Brown found that it was common for students to feel their personalities had changed in some way through the intercultural transition, and that as a result they would not fit as easily into their home cultures upon return. This experience was particularly salient for students from cultures more collectivistic than the British culture, who felt they had developed a sense of independence while in the UK that might be hard to integrate into their lives back home.[19] Spending time abroad can lead you to feel less comfortable with some of the norms in your own culture that you once took for granted. Studies of Japanese students and businesspeople returning home after an experience abroad, for example, have found that returnees often feel conflicted about customs around group-individual relations, assertiveness, and interactions between younger and older persons—all areas in which Japanese norms tend to differ from those of many Western cultures.[20]

For students who identify as part of a minority group at home, or who have felt marginalized because of their social identity in their home cultures, the feeling of being a "stranger" at home can take on a heightened significance. Depending on the host culture, students in this situation might feel they are more readily accepted while abroad than they often are at home, and this can bring a great deal of distress and questioning of one's social identity at home, making the transition difficult and even painful.[21] In other situations, though, students may encounter prejudice or racism in the host country in ways they have not experienced at home. This creates distress for the individual and can increase feelings of isolation and homesickness; some research suggests that it can also enhance students' empathy and compassion for others who are marginalized after the return home. This can be the case for majority-group students who have not been highly aware of prejudice in their home environments, but notice it more in the host culture and then retain this awareness after they return home.[22] In this case the transition can become, among other things, a period of reckoning, of questioning and newly examining injustices in one's home culture.

More generally, an experience abroad can highlight social roles and relations, bringing those things more into our awareness upon return home. In fact, several studies have suggested that students who spend time abroad often adopt a more person-oriented outlook, including heightened awareness of international and political concerns and greater interest in human nature generally.[23] We will turn to the impact of education abroad on one's global perspectives later in the book.

In the hallway: Considering Dana's experience

In the story that started this chapter, Dana is going through multiple transitions. For example, she is changing her major, which means ending her associations with one set of faculty and students, and beginning associations with another set of different people. This transition is taking place as a result of her new interest in designing her own major, something she realized she wanted to do while abroad in China. There is also the most obvious transition that Dana is experiencing: being home after being in China. One experience ended, another began at home, but both are connected, influenced by and influencing the other. A third transition is that she is moving out of the apartment that she shared with her roommate, as they no longer get along since she came back. The probable result of Dana moving out and no longer sharing a place with Nisha would be the ending of the friendship—another significant transition. A final possible transition you might infer from the story is that Dana would be living alone, perhaps for the first time.

Dana finds herself in flux, between two places, two majors, two ways of being. She is not quite comfortable in one or the other space, and she is anticipating the future with a mixture of excitement and nervousness. She probably feels some degree of disorientation, not quite sure of "where she is." But she feels confident enough about her choices to move forward, despite not knowing exactly what lies ahead. She is ready to take the next step, to shape her own path, and in doing so redefine herself to some degree.

So, you can see how Dana's experiences abroad and in reentry at home have resulted in major transitions in her life. In your own reentry experience, consider your recent experiences, and reflect on the transitions you have gone through, are going through, or may need to go through. This process of reflection will help you better understand your transition and feel more prepared to take the next step.

In the next chapter, we move from a focus on your individual transition experience to an interpersonal perspective, taking a look at the critical role of communication in reentry transitions.

Notes

1. Ingram, R., Field, J., & Gallacher, J. (2009). Learning transitions: Research, policy, practice. In J. Field, J. Gallacher, & R. Ingram (Eds.), *Researching Transitions in Lifelong Learning* (pp. 1–6). New York: Routledge. Quote p. 2.
2. Stephenson-Abetz, J. & Holman, A. (2012). Home is where the heart is: Facebook and the negotiation of "old" and "new" during the transition to college. *Western Journal of Communication*, 76(2), 175–193. Quote p. 175
3. Ingram, Field, & Gallacher (2009). Quote p. 2.
4. Sussman, N.M. (2002). Testing the cultural identity model of the cultural transition cycle: Sojourners return home. *International Journal of Intercultural Relations*, 26, 391–408.
5. Bridges, W. (2004). *Transitions: Making Sense of Life's Changes.* Cambridge, MA: Da Capo Press.
6. Basseches, M. (1984). *Dialectical Thinking and Adult Development.* Norwood, NJ: Ablex, p. 323.

7 Martin, J. & Harrell, T. (2004). Intercultural reentry of students and professionals: Theory and practice. In D. Landis, J. Bennett, & M. Bennett (Eds.), *Handbook of Intercultural Training* (pp. 309–332). Thousand Oaks, CA: Sage Publishing.
8 Hunley, H.A. (2010). Students' functioning while studying abroad: The impact of psychological distress and loneliness. *International Journal of Intercultural Relations, 34*(4), 386–392; Wielkiewicz, R.M. & Turkowski, L.W. (2010). Reentry issues upon returning from study abroad programs. *Journal of College Student Development, 51*(6), 649–664; Cockburn, L. (2002). Children and young people living in changing worlds: The process of assessing and understanding the "third culture kid." *School Psychology, 23*, 475–485; Gaw, K.F. (2000). Reverse culture shock in students returning from overseas. *International Journal of Intercultural Relations, 24*, 83–104.
9 Ecclestone, K. (2009). Lost and found in translation: Educational implications of concerns about 'identity', 'agency' and 'structure'. In J. Field, J. Gallacher, & R. Ingram (Eds.), *Researching Transitions in Lifelong Learning* (pp. 9–27). New York: Routledge.
10 Mezirow, J. (2000). Learning to think like an adult: Core concepts of transformation theory. In J. Mezirow & Associates (Eds.), *Learning as Transformation* (pp. 3–33). San Francisco, CA: Jossey-Bass; Jarvis, P. (2006). *Towards a Comprehensive Theory of Human Learning*. New York: Routledge.
11 Ecclestone (2009) p. 13.
12 Ecclestone (2009).
13 Sussman, N.M. (2000). The dynamic nature of cultural identity throughout cultural transitions: Why home is not so sweet. *Personality and Social Psychology Review, 4*(4), 355–373.
14 Sussman (2000); Huff, J. (2001). Parental attachment, reverse culture shock, perceived social support, and college adjustment of missionary children. *Journal of Psychology and Theology, 29*(3), 246–264.
15 Sussman, N.M. (2001). Repatriation transitions: Psychological preparedness, cultural identity, and attributions among American managers. *International Journal of Intercultural Relations, 25*, 109–123.
16 Rogers, J. & Ward, C. (1993). Expectation-experience discrepancies and psychological adjustment during cross-cultural reentry. *International Journal of Intercultural Intercultural Relations, 17*(2), 185–196.
17 Sussman (2001); Sussman, N.M. (2002). Testing the cultural identity model of the cultural transition cycle: Sojourners return home. *International Journal of Intercultural Relations, 26*, 391–408.
18 Kidder, L.H. (1992). Requirements for being "Japanese": Stories of returnees. *International Journal of Intercultural Relations, 16*(4), 383–393.
19 Brown, L. (2009). The transformative power of the international sojourn: An ethnographic study of the international student experience. *Annals of Tourism Research, 36*(3), 502–521.
20 Isogai, T., Hayashi, Y., & Uno, M. (1999). Identity issues and reentry training. *International Journal of Intercultural Relations, 23*(3), 493–525.
21 Gaw (2000).
22 Trilokekar, R.D. & Kukar, P. (2011). Disorienting experiences during study abroad: Reflections of pre-service teacher candidates. *Teaching and Teacher Education, 27*(7), 1141–1150; Talburt, S. & Stewart, M. (1999). What's the subject of study abroad?: Race, gender, and "living culture." *The Modern Language Journal, 83*(2), 163–175.
23 Ryan, M.E. & Twibell, R.S. (2000). Concerns, values, stress, coping, health, and educational outcomes of college students who studied abroad. *International Journal of Intercultural Relations, 24*(4), 409–435.

FOOD FOR THOUGHT

1. What has been the trajectory of your own cross-cultural experience and transition back home? How would you diagram it? Can you identify particular high and low points? Key junctures where you came to see something in a new light?
2. What are some decisions you have made—large or small—since returning home that have impacted your direction in school, in your career path, or in your personal life? How might those decisions have been affected by your experience abroad?
3. Has your self-concept been changed at all through your experience abroad? Do you see your own identity—and the ways in which your identity plays out in your environment—differently now, even in subtle ways?
4. How do you now perceive your own agency—your ability to create your own path in the world—as compared to before your time abroad? Has there been any change? If so, in what ways?

Suggestions for further reading

Bridges, W. (2004). *Transitions: Making Sense of Life's Changes*. Cambridge: MA: Da Capo Press.

Storti, C. (2001). *The Art of Coming Home*. Boston, MA: Intercultural Press.

Tennant, M. (2012). *The Learning Self: Understanding the Potential for Transformation*. San Francisco: Jossey-Bass.

6
COMMUNICATING IN REENTRY

CHAPTER OVERVIEW

In this chapter, we explore communication in reentry. Coming home from studying abroad provides students with both the opportunity and the challenge of articulating what their experience in the host culture means to them, and how or if they have changed. We'll provide information for you to consider and apply when engaging in communication with friends, family, peers, and professors during your transition back home.

Reentry fiction: What can I say?

Yolanda had been home in Durban for two months and still didn't know exactly what she wanted to say when people asked her about her study-abroad experience in England. She had, however, developed a shorthand version for people who asked her, "How was it?" In English or Afrikaans, she would say, "I enjoyed being at the university and being in Liverpool was fun. But, I hated the weather. Most of the people were nice, but some of their accents were very hard to understand." For most people, this was enough information, and Yolanda had learned not to expect too much more than an initial expression of interest from her friends.

Take Christo, her good friend from high school. She met him by chance at the mall a week after her return to South Africa. After hugging and exchanging greetings, he asked her about her "trip." She gave him her standard reply that she had already developed since being home. His response had been "Ja, that sounds cool. Those poms do sound funny. Our weather here's lekker, so no wonder you didn't like it there." The topic of conversation then moved on to her plans for the rest of the day and to some gossip about mutual friends she had not yet seen.

Christo's reaction to her news about her time studying abroad had been typical, especially from her friends. Yolanda was surprised at how they were not more curious about her education-abroad experiences, and didn't ask her many questions beyond their initial inquiry. She had been annoyed at first, then puzzled, and then a little hurt by their apparent lack of interest about her time in England. She also felt annoyed when people called her year away "a trip" (in English) or "vakaansie" (in Afrikaans), as if she had been on an extended vacation, instead of studying marine biology at the University of Liverpool.

There were of course some exceptions to this seemingly uninterested response, and Yolanda could always count on her best friend Nomvula to pepper her with questions about England and her time there. Nomvula had asked her about her courses, her flat, her roommates, how she got around, if she saw Big Ben, the Tower of London, Buckingham Palace, and where the Beatles used to play. It felt good to be able to talk in detail about her time away to someone who genuinely seemed interested. Yet still, Yolanda felt that Nomvula could not truly understand how much her time in Liverpool meant to her, and how she felt it had really changed her, and her life.

As Yolanda strolled down the road toward the beach to meet up with Nomvula and her boyfriend Deon, she pulled out her phone to check if either one had texted her. Yolanda had to admit to herself that part of the reason Nomvula could not fully grasp how much the time in England meant to her was that she couldn't fully explain it to herself yet. She knew she was changed by it, but could not really explain, clearly, in a way Nomvula would understand, exactly how she'd been changed or why. She could catch glimpses of her changed self, but they felt a bit like a dream that she could not quite recall, and would take time to fully realize. Her phone chimed in her hand, and she shielded the screen from the glare of the sun to see who had sent her a text message.

REENTERING STUDENT QUOTES

- "You can't always express how it made you feel. You can say what you did, what you saw, what you ate, people you met. However, putting into words—the way it made you feel about yourself, your place in the world, and the world around you—is much harder to convey and to put into a concrete set of words and ideas."
- "I have concluded that no one will ever really understand my experiences abroad, and that's OK."
- "I generally exclude the part where I feel like I'm still recovering from my experience from a year ago, because that requires more explanation."

Communication is key

A student's sense of changed cultural identity, their preference for a new style of clothing or music, their use of a second language, their expression of emotion and sense of alienation, all of those are channeled through communication in reentry. Part of what we want to do in this book is provide you with ways to effectively communicate about the whole cycle of your experience, including reentry. It might be communication with yourself (intrapersonal communication), your friends, family, peers, teachers, and counselors (interpersonal communication, mediated communication) or communication with classmates in discussions and presentations (small group, public communication). Reflecting on your verbal and nonverbal expressions can help you manage and negotiate your reentry, and process your study-abroad experiences.

Intercultural expert Young Yun Kim[1] suggests that we think of people as being open systems. People, as open systems, are connected to the environments in which they live, and they relate to those environments through the process of communication. So, she argues, it is through the communication process that people learn culture. In addition, communicative competence has been found to be a significant factor in explaining returnee adjustment.[2]

Intercultural researcher and theorist Shelley Smith[3] proposed a model to help us understand reentry. Her model links the ideas of identity, reentry adjustment, and intercultural communication competence. A very interesting claim she makes is that for some returnees, the identity change that has taken place due to their adjustment during their time abroad makes "communication between returnees and members of their home culture (at times) *intercultural*."[4] What do you think of this idea? Have there been times since you returned home when you have felt like people do not "get you" anymore, that they do not understand you, that you cannot express what you are thinking and feeling effectively? If so, then this idea, that sometimes communication back home in reentry can feel like intercultural communication (communication taking place between people from different cultures) may be a useful frame to consider.

Smith[5] further suggests that when returnees reenter, they engage in a kind of renegotiation about where they fit in back home. This renegotiation is tied to identity negotiation, and according to her model, intercultural communication competence. In other words, when you come home, you have to be able to communicate effectively about your experience abroad and be able to articulate clearly and specifically your new sense of identity. If you can manage this communication process effectively, she claims it may "lead to improved relationships, greater social and emotional support, and ultimately the refinement of one's intercultural identity and that identity's orientation to the home culture."[6] As you can see, communication is indeed key to a successful reentry experience. There are, however, different kinds of communication students engage in when back home. Next we will consider how students summarize their education-abroad experience for others.

The "elevator speech"

We have found in our own experiences that once we got home from a significant intercultural sojourn, we developed a short answer to respond to questions from family, friends, and acquaintances who ask about out time in the host culture. Through our interactions over the years with students who have studied abroad, and through research we have conducted, it is clear that students share this experience—coming up with a "short version" speech to provide a summary description of their study-abroad experiences to others.

Please take a moment to consider the following questions:

- Have you developed such an "elevator speech" in reentry? If so, what does it include?
- How did you decide what to say and what to leave out of your "elevator speech?"
- Does your "elevator speech" change at all for different friends or family?

Take a few minutes to write down some answers to these questions before moving on to consider the information below.

Students often talk about the following ideas in those short-version replies to the common "*How was it abroad*?" question they face upon reentry from well-meaning and often interested people in their lives:

- **Difficulty:** Students describe facing some difficulties during their experience, like culture shock or adjustment issues.
- **Loneliness:** Students discuss being lonely or bored when abroad.
- **Novelty:** Students talk about new experiences in the host culture.
- **Recommendations:** Students urge others to study abroad or to travel.
- **Relationships:** Students describe connections made with people in the host culture that are meaningful to the student.
- **Returning:** Students talk about wanting to repeat the experience or longing to have been able to stay longer.[7]

Do you see, in the list above, any themes that you include in your short answer to people's initial inquiries about your experience in the host culture?

Below are some examples of what actual students have said in response to the "*How was it abroad*?" question:

> "Amazing. The most impactful experience of my life. I have meaningful relationships with Salvadoran & US students alike."
>
> "I learned a lot about the subject I wanted to study (chemistry and the atmosphere), but felt very lonely and was bored often."
>
> "It was the best experience of my life. And everyone should go to Florence with Gonzaga."

"It was good, but I wish I had stayed longer and was more immersed in the culture during my time there."

"The food and wine were amazing, and the country was beautiful."

How does your elevator speech compare to these students' versions? From relationships, to feelings, to general claims about their time in the host culture, these student examples provide you with a sample of how students might summarize their long, complex experience abroad in short form.

Do I mean it?

You now know something about the content of what some returnees include in their elevator speeches when communicating in reentry. We think it is useful to also consider motivation. That is, motivation for the inclusion of some information, and the exclusion of other information about students' experiences in the host culture. In a study we ran on reentering students' experience, we found that often, their short description of their study-abroad experience *was* actually what they wanted people to know about their experience. Four common reasons to explain how and why this is the case include:

- **Desire to tell the truth:** Some students reported that their short descriptions were true and represented how they honesty felt about their study-abroad experiences. "I actually loved it," they might say, or "My short speech is as honest as possible given that it is supposed to be short."
- **Desire to give only partial information:** It was reported that the short descriptions represented one part of the international sojourn. For example, one student said, "It's fine for the short version, but not wholly representative of my experience and time spent there."
- **Desire to possibility share more detail**: Students suggested that there might be more detail about the sojourn that they may share with people later or if asked. One student commented, "If they have specific questions, I'll answer them, but otherwise I don't want to bombard [people] with unnecessary information."
- **Desire to have a positive focus:** A number of students focused on the positive elements of their study-abroad experiences. A student told us, for instance, "…my explanation is brief so I really only focus on the good things," and another said, "Of course I am not going to get into the crazy, scary, sad, or rough experiences of studying abroad right off the bat…"[8]

On the other hand, there were also returnees who say that their short description *was not* what they really would like to tell people about their time abroad. Five common reasons given to explain how and why this is the case include:

- **Articulation:** Some students found it difficult to explain the significance/importance of the study-abroad experience. As one student put it, "…this is difficult to put into words," and another, "…it's also hard to articulate how much of a life-changing experience study abroad was for me."
- **Challenges:** Students also talked about challenges they faced in the host culture. For instance, one confided, "…there were ups and downs and there are tough parts about learning to live in another country/culture," and another, "…it was great but also very hard."
- **Conversation target:** Some students reported that they could talk to friends easily in more depth about their experiences, but not so with acquaintances. The target of conversation changed what a student might say. Comments included "I'd say yes and no because it depends on the individual I'm speaking with. If it's someone I consider close, the short elevator speech is not enough" and "…not everyone wants to hear about the negative experiences of studying abroad."
- **Study-abroad program:** Students described negative aspects of the specific study-abroad *program* (not the host culture). An example of this is "I also have a lot of criticisms about my particular program," or "I didn't get along with a lot of the other students in the program."
- **Time:** Some students described not having enough time in a conversation to explain or talk about everything the student might want to about their sojourn. One said, "…it would take a while to explain and show it all," and another, "its hard to explain six months in two minutes."[9]

In reading the themes presented above, do any resonate with you? Do you really tell people what you want them to know about your experiences in the host culture, or do you tell them what you think they want to hear? Can you see your motivations for your communicative choices in any of these themes?

Are you heard?

So what kind of responses might students expect to receive from friends and family who listen to their short-version speech? What sort of responses have you had? There are a variety of responses returnees might get in talking about their study-abroad experience during reentry. In our research, four main response themes were common:

- **Excitement:** People often express some level of excitement when a respondent tells them about their experience abroad. This excitement may be expressed rather superficially with "cool," "awesome," "wow," and "great" being the most commonly reported responses. But this excitement was also reported as being genuinely expressed.

- **Interest:** Students reported that people showed interest in their experiences by asking questions about their time abroad.
- **Envy:** Students said that people frequently demonstrated some level of envy when being told about the study-abroad experience. One student described this type of "jealousy" most accurately as "good-natured envy."
- **Positive feedback:** Students frequently said that the people they told of their experience abroad responded positively in some fashion, saying they were happy for the student.[10]

There are a range of ways in which people in your life might respond to your communicating about your study-abroad experience. This is normal. It is well worth spending some time in reentry thinking, in specific terms, about specific people to whom you have talked about your experiences. Does your best friend react differently than a casual acquaintance when you talk to them about your time in the host culture? Have your parents expressed any interest in hearing about your time away or how you are doing now that you are home? Do professors in your classes seem to appreciate your insights gained through studying abroad when you share those in class discussions?

Communication starting points

One piece of communication advice we'd give is to talk more about your time in the host culture and your transition home with those people whose responses meet your needs, and less with those who don't. This may seem like simple advice, but in reality it is not. We generally want people we feel close with to help us meet our needs. It is disappointing when they do not. However, in the reentry transition, given the unique nature of your own experiences abroad and at home, sometimes those we usually feel the most close to, cannot easily relate to our thoughts and feelings. This is especially true if they have never spent time in another culture of any significant length or immersion. Finding people to talk to who seem to "get it" is important, and will help you (and them) gain from the conversations in which you engage.

Another communication starting point we think is well worth considering is to talk about different elements of the experience abroad and your reentry transition with different people. Take some of *their* interests into consideration in picking what information to share and what not to share. Sometimes, given the excitement, confusion, challenges, and new insights a returnee is experiencing, their communication might appear to others to be very self-focused, and very narrow in scope. (This is not surprising considering returnees are often working out identity-related issues during their reentry, which however might seem a bit tedious, repetitive, and self-centered when viewed from another's perspective.) Finding common ground, and considering the audience of your communication, is important in helping make your communication more effective and satisfying for all involved.

Campus communication

Returnees do not only communicate with friends and family about their time spent abroad. There are also contexts and opportunities on campus for speaking about time in the host culture and about the reentry transition. Researcher Dennis Doyle[11] suggests that the "campus community rarely gets a good sense about how students grow and change during their semester(s) studying abroad."

When we asked, many returning students said they would be willing to share or present their experiences from their time studying abroad in some way on campus. Students have different reasons as to why they would be willing to do this. Below are some examples of what returning students have said as to why they'd be willing to engage in this campus communication:

> "I would love to just talk to people about my experience abroad. It is one of my favorite things to talk about. I love to share my pictures."
>
> "I would love to talk to people who are thinking of going abroad, and help find programs that would suit them. Also to provide support while they're abroad, offering myself as a connection to the US to figure out logistical things."
>
> "I would tell people at various events to really put themselves out there in the world in an effort to become a more well-rounded person."

On the other hand, some students do *not* really want to share their study-abroad experiences with others on the campus when they get home. This is fine. As one student put it when asked about this opportunity, "I wouldn't want to present my experience." Another student was more blunt, "Nope!" Still other students might not be so emphatic or so sure that they do not want to discuss their experiences with others on campus. As an American student from Seattle stated, "I am not sure I would be interested in sharing." Another student suggested, "I don't know that I would share my experiences in an official format or presentation, I'd rather get coffee with someone that is interested in studying abroad in a program like mine or in Prague."

Remember that sharing the experiences you had abroad and your experiences once back home may help you process your thinking about this transition. A student in reentry cannot talk clearly to others about these experiences unless they have reflected carefully on what they want to say. Agreeing to talk to others, then, might be helpful not only for those whom returnees speak to, but for themselves as well.

Students have a wide range of preferences for sharing information. The options range from formal presentations with slides to a large audience in a public setting like a classroom or auditorium, to informal one-on-one conversations with other students interested in studying abroad at a coffee shop. We would urge you to consider these options as a way to share both the reentry challenges you might be facing and to explore the multiple positive benefits that studying abroad provides once back home again.

What does the research say?

Researcher Yuliya Kartoshkina[12] found an interesting way to describe reentry from a phrase that several of the students who were part of her research used: bittersweet. Part of the bitter-sweetness of reentry according to the returning students comes from communication. The bitter, in part, was because students perceived that they could *not* effectively communicate with people back home about their intercultural experiences—this was especially true of people who had not had a significant intercultural experience themselves. The sweet, in part, was because students perceived that they could effectively communicate with people back home about their intercultural experiences with people who had themselves had a significant intercultural experience.

The research supports the idea that students often have trouble expressing themselves articulately as to the value of their study-abroad experiences once they get home: as Doyle has written, "When asked to put their experiences studying abroad into words, students usually can only respond with such unsatisfying phrases as 'it was great, life-changing,' or the truly vacuous 'it was awesome.'"[13] Being able to effectively communicate their experiences abroad to their family and friends back home in reentry is hard, and is one specific area of communication competence that has been found lacking in returning students.[14]

Another challenge to communicating in reentry can be a new skepticism for one's home culture communication style. For example, Laura Sicola[15] found that "re-entrants did express surprise at people's displays of previously accepted 'home culture' communication styles, and uncertainty about how to interact with other Americans upon re-entry." One of the students in Sicola's study,[16] for instance—an American reentering after a sojourn in Zimbabwe—"described Zimbabwean greetings as 'long and drawn out', whereas in the US 'we don't even go through the motions.'"

Similarly, intercultural researchers Tomoko Isogai, Yuko Hayashi, and Mayumi Uno[17] report that Japanese returnees experienced interpersonal problems based largely around communication connected to and reflected in cultural values. Examples of communication challenges they discuss include that Japanese returnees may be perceived as being too direct in their communication style, violating Japanese cultural preferences for indirectness at times, the specific challenge of not being able to say "no" to people directly, and having to be very vigilant to nonverbal communication elements in ways they did not have to be when in the host culture.

Language issues can also cause challenges for returnees. For example, Tomoko Yoshida and six research colleagues[18] found that Japanese returnees had language-related issues and issues related to bilingualism upon reentry. Specifically, young Japanese returnees reported that people back home expected them to be fluent in English because of their time in host cultures. Second, there was a perception that returnees' fluency in the Japanese language was not as effective as it might have been expected to be by those in the home culture

In another study done on returnees to New Zealand after significant intercultural experiences in different European Union host cultures, Natalia Chaban[19] and her four research colleagues found that returnees reported reentry elation and reentry shock. The elation stage was early on in the transition, and the shock phase followed. Key to these phases were positive and negative communication experiences. For example, positive communication experiences for returnees included people being very interested in hearing their stories about their time in the host culture, wanting to look at their photos from abroad, and having a generally warm and welcoming tenor to the interpersonal communication (if not a full understanding or grasp of the returnees' experiences). In contrast, in the shock phase, returnees reported interpersonal communication adjustments from simple nonverbal greeting behavior (like kissing hello or shaking hands) to not having current cultural references at hand (since time away from New Zealand meant time away from current cultural happenings and references).

Clearly, it is important to pay close attention to how you, as a reentering student, communicate about your experiences abroad and in reentry. Also, considering wisely the targets of your communication—in other words, thinking about to whom you want to talk about your experiences—is vital. As a returnee, you would be well served to select people to share information with who will be receptive to and supportive of that communication.

Further, research connected to transitions and lifelong learning tells us that people "more adept at engaging in processes of telling stories about their lives than others" may vary as well in their potential for personal development through communication).[20] Your capacity to tell your stories, both about your time abroad and your reentry transition, may aid in the amount you can learn from those experiences.

What can I say? Considering Yolanda's experience

From our story at the beginning of the chapter, there are a number of ideas to consider when thinking about Yolanda's communication interactions since she got back to South Africa from England. Like many students, she had a canned version of what to tell people about her experience. She included positive and negative elements, and told people the truth. The information she gave them was enough to satisfy an initial inquiry by friends and family as to how her time studying abroad was, and she had practiced it in two languages (English and Afrikaans).

The communication problem from Yolanda's perspective was that her short speech provided ample chance for people to ask other questions about her experience, but many did not take that opportunity, illustrated by her friend Christo in the story. For example, you might expect someone to reply "What were their accents like that made those people in Liverpool so hard to understand?" A question like that from a friend would show Yolanda their interest, and allow her the chance to talk more about her experience. Her range of feelings (annoyed, puzzled, hurt) came about because she perceived their lack of interest in her experience as a lack of interest in or care for her.

If this is something you have experienced, consider how you have chosen to deal with that situation. Yolanda had a friend, Nomvula, whom she could count on to talk to, in detail, about her time abroad and what it was like to be home again. Students in reentry need to make sure that there are some people in their lives to whom they can happily and freely talk about both the good and bad experiences abroad and at home.

Often, those who have had similar experiences (like other students who have studied abroad, or people who have traveled a lot) are good listeners and are genuinely interested in hearing about returnees' time away. Remembering the reentry styles we read about earlier in the book, you should make sure you are not constantly denigrating your home culture, nor constantly talking about how wonderful your host culture is either. Striking a balance is needed.

In communicating with friends, family, classmates, teachers, and people in their workplaces, you may, either explicitly or implicitly, be managing your relationships. In the next chapter, considering relationships in reentry after having studied abroad will be our focus.

Notes

1 Kim, Y.Y. (2000). *Becoming Intercultural: An Integrative Theory of Communication and Cross-cultural Adaptation*. Thousand Oaks, CA: Sage.
2 Moriyoshi, N. (2001). *What Is Adjustment? The Adjustment Process of Japanese Returnee Children*. Doctoral dissertation, University of Pennsylvania, USA. (Unpublished).
3 Smith, S. (2001). An identity model of reentry communication competence. *World Communication*, *30*(3/4), 6–38.
4 Smith (2001). Quote p. 6.
5 Smith (2001).
6 Smith (2001). Quote p. 9.
7 Malleus, R. (2015). *Embracing Opportunity: Students Communicating in Intercultural Reentry*. National Communication Association conference. Las Vegas, NV.
8 Malleus (2015).
9 Malleus (2015).
10 Malleus (2015).
11 Doyle, D. (2009). Holistic assessment and the study abroad experience. *Frontiers: The Interdisciplinary Journal of Study Abroad*, *18*, 143–155. Quote p. 144.
12 Kartoshkina, Y. (2015). Bittersweet reentry after studying abroad. *International Journal of Intercultural Relations*, *44*, 35–45.
13 Doyle (2009). Quote p. 144.
14 Neuliep, J.W. (2009). *Intercultural Communication: A Contextual Approach*. Thousand Oaks, CA: Sage.
15 Sicola, L. (2005). 'Communicative lingerings': Exploring awareness of L2 influence on L1 in American expatriates after re-entry. *Language Awareness*, *14*(2/3), 153–169. Quote p. 166.
16 Sicola (2005). Quote p. 162.
17 Isogai, T.Y., Hayashi, Y., & Uno, M. (1999). Identity issues and reentry training. *International Journal of Intercultural Relations*, *23*(3), 493–525.

18 Yoshida, T., Matsumoto, D., Akashi, S., Akiyama, T., Furiuye, A., Ishii, C., & Moriyoshi, N. (2009). Contrasting experiences in Japanese returnee adjustment: Those who adjust easily and those who do not. *International Journal of Intercultural Relations, 33*(4), 265–276.
19 Chaban, N., Williams, A., Holland, M., Boyce, V., & Warner, F. (2011). Crossing-cultures: Analysing the experiences of NZ returnees from the EU (UK vs. non-UK). *International Journal of Intercultural Relations, 35*, 776–790.
20 Tedder, M. & Biesta, G. (2009). Biography, transition and learning in the lifecourse: The role of narrative. In J. Field, J. Gallacher, & R. Ingram (Eds.), *Researching Transitions in Lifelong Learning* (pp. 76–90). New York: Routledge. Quote p. 77.

FOOD FOR THOUGHT

1. What topics are present in your reentry "elevator speech"? Can you relate any of those topics to the themes discussed in this chapter?
2. If you were offered a chance to talk, on campus, to an audience about your study-abroad and reentry experiences, what would be the three main ideas you would present and why?
3. Are there any specific ways of communicating (verbal and nonverbal) in your host culture that you miss now that you are back home? If so, why, and if not, why not?

Suggestions for further reading

Kartoshkina, Y. (2015). Bittersweet reentry after studying abroad. *International Journal of Intercultural Relations, 44*, 35–45.

Smith, S. (2001). An identity model of reentry communication competence. *World Communication, 30*(3/4), 6–38.

Storti, C. (1994). *Cross-cultural Dialogues: 74 Brief Encounters with Cultural Difference.* Boston, MA: Intercultural Press.

7
REDEFINING RELATIONSHIPS

CHAPTER OVERVIEW

In this chapter, we look at the nature of your relationships—both in your host culture and in your home culture—and how those may have changed over time. We'll consider the kinds of relationships you've had in both places, what you are looking for in your relationships, and what kind of orientation you might have to friendship. We'll also think about different kinds of relationships—friends, families, romantic partners—and reflect on what you can do to make the most of the relationships that are important to you at home and abroad.

Reentry fiction: The birthday party

She sat quietly in the corner of the room as conversation swirled around her. It was her grandmother's eightieth birthday celebration, and all her relatives and family friends were there. Lin-Lee had been home in Taiwan for a couple of months now, but she just couldn't seem to slot herself back into her old place in the family. Like today, when her younger sister Tan had prepared the table settings for the party—that had *always* been Lin-Lee's job before! She shouldn't be angry with her sister, but there was a part of her that felt really annoyed.

Lin-Lee had nodded and smiled when her uncle and aunt were talking about what a wonderful wedding her cousin had had six months ago, and she'd felt left out when her mom giggled remembering the gaffe the groom's boss had made when making his speech. So much had happened at home during the year she had been abroad studying. Lin-Lee had seen the wedding pictures posted on Instagram, and had read the Facebook posts from her sister and cousins, but it was not the same as being at the wedding.

Lin-Lee's grandmother, eyes sparkling with happiness at being surrounded by her family, approached her. She smiled gently down at Lin-Lee and thanked her, for the third time, for the lovely gift Lin-Lee had given her. Lin-Lee knew that she was her grandmother's favorite grandchild, even though the elderly woman would never admit it, and was glad that at least *that* had not changed while she had been gone.

Walking toward a group of young women, her cousins, and Tan, Lin-Lee almost diverted to the kitchen instead of joining them. "This is silly," she thought to herself. "These people are my family, my friends—why do I feel so out of place?" She joined the circle of chatting women and managed to hold up her end of the conversation. She was pleasantly surprised when she noticed that the time had flown by, and that she'd actually had fun.

The last plate was washed, and Tan was drying it. Lin-Lee rinsed the soap off her hands and quietly asked her sister the question she'd been dying to bring up for days now. "Do you think I've changed a lot since I went away to university?" Laughing, Tan replied, "You're quieter now, and not so bossy to me!" Then, seeing that Lin-Lee was serious, Tan added, "I don't think you're very different, but you do not seem as sure of yourself as before you went away. Maybe you just need time to settle down, to get used to us all again. Are you not happy to be home?" "No, no," Lin-Lee hastily answered, "of course I'm happy to be home. But you're right, I do need some time to get used to things here again."

Later, she could hear Tan's breathing, slow and steady, and she knew her sister was asleep. The sound was comforting to Lin-Lee, who had shared a bedroom with Tan all her life, apart from her year away. They'd whispered together for an hour tonight before Tan had fallen asleep, just like when they were kids.

The apartment seemed so quiet now, after the noise of celebration that the party had brought earlier in the day. It had, after all, been good to see the family again. The awkward moments of searching for things to say to people you haven't seen or talked to in-person over a year had eased a bit. She really couldn't believe that her newly married cousin was already expecting a baby!

Tan muttered in her sleep, and Lin-Lee realized that it wasn't only she who had changed since she'd been away; her baby sister had matured a lot, too. Tan had a boyfriend (although their parents did *not* know about him and they only met each other with other friends, in a group). She did more work around the apartment without being nagged by their mother. She didn't bother Lin-Lee with questions about every decision she had to make, ranging from which dress to wear for some occasion to what qualities she should look for in a husband. Still, as Lin-Lee drifted off to sleep, she happily decided they were still close, even after her year abroad.

REENTERING STUDENT QUOTES

➤ "I've suffered a set-back in the closeness of my family. I often feel left out, and sometimes even alienated, in my own home. They feel like I'm 'above them' now, and not interested in their lives."

> "Being abroad enabled me to make new friends, who can now share that experience with me. But many of my friendships at home have changed, some for the better and some for the worse."
>
> "I realize now that I can depend on my family in any instance. I am closer to family members and true friends."

Relationship inventory

Let's start off with some statements to consider, thinking about which is most true for you:

a. Since returning home from my overseas experience, I feel closer to my friends and family than I did before.
b. Since returning home, I feel more alienated from friends and family.
c. I really feel no difference in my closeness to friends and family.

If you answered (c), you might count yourself as one of the lucky returnees with relatively stable post-experience relationships. If you answered either (a) or (b), however, count yourself as one among many whose relationships change, sometimes dramatically, after a profound intercultural experience like studying abroad in a host culture.

Consider the following examples:

Example One: Tony had a few very close friends throughout college. He and his friends often spent time discussing issues important to them, and he felt that they knew each other quite well. While he was away in Japan, two of his good friends were also away on overseas experiences. When Tony returned home, he found he was able to talk openly about his experience with his friends, and he felt that they understood what it had meant to him. He had changed, but he knew they had changed, too, and it didn't seem to pose a problem in their friendship. In fact, Tony felt it may have strengthened their friendship by enabling them to "keep pace" with one another and get to know one another better.

Example Two: Monica went to college in her hometown and was able to maintain friendships with a group of friends from high school. The group often socialized together, and the members of the group shared a lot: friends, interests, and a childhood history. When Monica heard about a program to spend a year in Spain, she found she was the only one of her group of friends to be interested. She decided to go, and while she was there, she maintained contact with many of her friends through social media and texting, so she was very surprised at the way she felt when she returned home. Suddenly she felt she had much less in common with these friends, and she found herself missing the friends she had made while overseas. She tried to share her experience of living in a foreign culture with some of her friends back home but felt frustrated when they seemed not really to understand what she meant. She had the sense that they were "stuck" in the everyday concerns that didn't seem as important to her anymore. She longed for people who could share her thoughts and understand her feelings.

Example Three: Mai had always been close to her family and felt she could share most things with her parents. In the weeks before her return home from Austria, she was excited to tell them all about her experience. When she arrived home, her parents listened to her stories and scrolled through some of the photos on her iPad, but she had the sense that they were growing weary of her frequent anecdotes and comments about the differences between "there" and "here." Once or twice, they even remarked that she seemed to think it was better "there," or that it was about time for her to get back to "real life." She felt frustrated and sometimes resentful of their lack of interest in her experience.

Example Four: Paul, a fourth-year student who had spent the past year in Kenya, looked forward to his return home. He had kept in close touch with his family and friends on Skype and through social media, and felt almost as if they had been there with him at times. In fact, he had the sense that his trip had actually brought him closer to his family. During his trip, he noticed—more than he ever had before—that they really supported him and showed interest in what he was doing. After he returned home, he felt a new appreciation for his family, especially for the security he felt in knowing he could always depend on them.

Each of these four people had different experiences coming back to friends and family because of a multitude of factors. Many returnees happily report that they feel stronger emotional ties to family, and to good friends, than before their departure. Others, though, have a harder time, feeling that their friends and family no longer understand them very well.

Why would there be two such diverse reactions? Your experience with relationships depends on many factors, including the kinds of relationships you had before you left, the kinds of relationships you had in your host country, how you felt about your experience, and how your friends and family felt about you going away.

Relationship reflections

As you think about your reentry experience with friends and family members, consider the following questions:

- **What were your relationships with friends and family like before you left?** Often, students who have historically had very close relationships to their families remain close through the intercultural experience. But sometimes, family members are confused by the changes in the returnee, and this can cause relationships to become more distant, at least for a time. Much the same is true in regard to friendships: friends sometimes see the returnee as having changed and aren't sure how to "relate" to him or her anymore. By the same token, returnees often feel their friends are "stuck" in old habits and interests and don't appreciate the new ones the returnee has brought home. It's not uncommon, in fact, for returnees to admit to feeling superior to their friends and family members who haven't had an overseas experience. If you find yourself feeling that way, it is helpful to first remember that you're not the only one, and then continually remind yourself that each person's accumulated experiences are unique. Realize that you now have insights that others may not have; however, friends and family too, as a result of their life experiences, see many things you do not.

- **To what extent did you *want* to be independent of friends or family before and during your trip?** Different people desire different degrees of independence from those around them. Often, students decide to take an overseas trip in part *because* they want to feel more independent of family and friends. If this was the case for you, you may find that you feel somewhat alienated from those friends and family afterwards. Or you may have conflicting feelings, at times wanting to share your experience and at other times wanting to keep it separate from them. This is all part of the process of adjustment, of making the transition from who you were before your intercultural experience to who you are now, and who you will be in the future.

- **How much intercultural or travel experience have your friends and family members had themselves?** If a reentering student has family and friends who have traveled quite a bit (or even moved around their own country), they probably have a good sense of what it is like to encounter different ways of life. The student may find that their family understands what they are experiencing better than others do. This understanding often also comes through other kinds of transition experiences that require people to adjust to different ways of thinking. Somebody who has made a major change in career fields, for example, may find it easy to relate to a returnee's intercultural experience.

- **What kinds of relationships did you develop in your host country?** Because notions of friendship differ from culture to culture, students living abroad often develop friendships that are different in important ways from the ones they had at home. For example, in some European cultures, friendships tend to develop slowly, but once you "break the friendship barrier," you are warmly welcomed into the circle of family and friends. In the United States, by contrast, friendships are often made easily and quickly, but casual friends do not generally become a part of one's long-lasting networks. Students who find themselves in this situation—having felt connected to a large group in the host country—may feel disappointed to return home to the more informal, less close-knit style of friendship common in the US.

Even if you find your friends and family don't seem to accept the changes you've undergone, don't feel that they *never* will. Change is hard, and it often takes people a long time to adjust to major change—even when it's somebody else's. You may find that this is especially true for your friends, who may themselves, too, undergo a lot of change in the coming years.

You should also remember that your friends and family have undergone their own change in the time you were away. They have had their own experiences, made their own new friends, grown in their own ways. It's as important for you to recognize and respect this as it is for them to understand the changes you have been through.

As a general rule of thumb, developmental theories tell us that people tend to develop a stronger sense of their own identity, and to feel more self-reliant and independent, as they move out of their teen years—approximately the 17-to-21-year-old time frame.[1] (Keep in mind that this varies, and that it will not necessarily be uniform across cultures.) If this is your age range, you may be feeling especially uncertain about any drifting you feel from your family, because you may only recently have begun to feel a real sense of independence from them. So it makes sense that you might feel unsettled, and maybe even conflicted, by any new division or differences you perceive between you and your family.

Whether you are feeling this way or not, here are some things you can do to help bridge the gap between the friends and family you left before you went abroad, and the "new you":

- **Share your genuine feelings about your experience abroad, warts and all.** It's great to share the fun you had, and the new and interesting things you learned while abroad, but with close family or friends, keep it real by talking about the challenges you faced, too. Did you struggle to understand employees at the grocery store? Feel embarrassed when you didn't know how to appropriately greet others? Sometimes feel lonely? It's OK to tell your full story to people you trust. It will help them understand your experience better, and show them that you're wanting to share your new experience fully with them.
- **Find others to talk to who understand the tension you're experiencing between the "old gang" and the "new you."** Friends who have also spent time abroad, or who have had other kinds of experiences that pull them out of their familiar environments, will be more likely to understand your situation and feelings. They may even be able to shed light on what you are experiencing and offer useful suggestions.
- **Be careful about slipping into condescension.** Sometimes, students who return from an experience abroad can develop a chip on their shoulders about having studied, volunteered, or worked internationally. They can tend to view old friends who haven't had that experience as naive or less cosmopolitan. Taking this approach leaves others thinking that you're looking down on them, which doesn't do a lot for a relationship. Be respectful, remember that they've also grown and developed while you were away, and be willing to learn from them, too. This can help you appreciate the privilege you've enjoyed in participating in an education-abroad experience—something that few people in the world get to do.

- **Be curious about others.** Life has gone on while you've been away. Friends have been in relationships, taken classes, started jobs, and had a whole host of other experiences. Likewise, your family members have had their own ups and downs, learned new things, and changed in their own right. Show interest in these things, in how others have been and what they have done while you were away. When you're the one who has been away and returns, it's natural that you get more of the attention. This is great at first, but keep in mind that after a while, it can feel tiresome to friends and family. Take an interest in them and signal that you know it's not all about you.
- **Give them (and yourself) room and time.** Relationships change, and it can take a while to get accustomed to a new pattern or new definitions within relationships. You and the other people involved need time to figure out where your relationship is, so to speak, and how you want to reshape it for the future. Take it easy, give yourself and others a break for the occasional awkward moment, and know that what you are experiencing is very much to be expected.

What is friendship, anyway?

It may be useful here to step back and consider what makes for a good friendship. With the significant transition of coming home after time away, it can be hard to clearly define for yourself what you are really looking for in your friends—and you may be looking for different things in different relationships. Friendship is important for everybody, and this can be especially so if you're a young adult, when you are likely to be spending a fairly large portion of your time socializing with friends and deriving a lot of your satisfaction from friendships.[2] There are many different ways to think about the purposes and impacts of friendship, and researchers have developed theories about friendship using different lenses on what it is as a phenomenon.[3] You could look at friendship as providing a reward or benefit for each person, as simply making us feel good when we are with the other person. Or you could look at friendship in terms of the exchange of value that each person provides for the other. If you feel you are getting out of the friendship what you expect, that it offers more than other possible friendships, and that you getting out of it what you put into it, you are likely to feel satisfied with the relationship. Or, you might look at friendship in terms of the agreeable sense of balance that exists between or among people who share perceptions about the outside world, and their efforts to maintain that balance. Finally, you can think about friendships in terms of the steps by which they develop, and sometimes, fade.

Take a few minutes to consider the friendships you have, both friends from home and friends you may have made abroad, and how you currently feel about them in terms of:

- How much you simply enjoy your interactions

- Other benefits you might feel from the relationship—intellectual development, practical guidance, exposure to new ideas or people
- The similarity or difference in your perspectives about real-world concerns
- How the friendship has changed over time, and where it might go from here

As you consider these things, keep in mind that no friendship provides everything, and it can be very fulfilling to have different kinds of relationships with different people. Remember, too, that friendships may have changed, but that doesn't mean they're not valuable any longer. If that's the case for you, you may need to redefine what the friendship means to you—and that takes time.

What is your orientation to friendship?

There are many different models and theories that can help us understand how different people experience friendships and other kinds of relationships. Sociologist Janice McCabe has developed a model based on many years of research which focuses on university students, and which might help you reflect on your friendships before, during, and after your time abroad.[4] McCabe describes three different approaches to friendship. As you read them, see if any of the characteristics ring true for you. Keep in mind, though, that there are other ways to think about friend relationships, and you may not fit neatly into any category:

1. **Tight-knitters,** or people who have a group of friends in which each member knows every other member (or nearly so). These tight-knit friend networks can be really helpful in providing support to their members, but on the flip side, they don't usually allow for a lot of fresh perspectives to come into the group.
2. **Compartmentalizers,** or people who have various small networks of friends, and members of the various networks don't necessarily know each other. This might be the case, for example, if you have a group of friends from your residence hall, a group from a club you're a part of, and a group from a job you have. The advantage here is that you have groups that you can move in and out of for different purposes and be exposed to a variety of ideas, but you wouldn't have the same sense of "tightness" as with the previous model.
3. **Samplers,** or those who have a number of close friendships with individual people, but those individuals aren't necessarily connected in any way. The upside here is that you are likely to have a sense of freedom and independence in your decision-making, activities, and so on; the downside *can* at times be a sense of isolation.

Do you recognize yourself in any of these three styles? If you're somebody who has tended to want a close-knit friendship group, it may be hard to suddenly feel removed from them. If this is the case for you, you might think about how you can share your new perspectives and ideas with those individuals you are closest to. You might also think about connecting with others not in that tight-knit group who share your perspectives or experiences. Are there groups you can get involved in, volunteering you could do, or other activities where you'd have the opportunity to make those connections? Finally, if you have developed new friendships as a result of your experience abroad, you might think of them as a new opportunity to develop close ties, and to branch out from—but not abandon—your traditional network.

If, on the other hand, you have tended to have clusters of friends, each cluster with its own "personality," then you might want to think about whether one or more of those clusters is a group where you can share and connect with others around your new perspectives and interests. If not, you might look for additional opportunities to do that, through courses, programming in your university, and so on.

And finally, if you have generally had individual relationships with friends who may not know one another well, you might want to consider leveraging your "returnee status" to explore connecting to a group—a student group, a language group, a club, or another type of organization—that focuses on international or similar issues of interest to you.

Whatever your friendships look like, returning home after time abroad will have some impact on your relationships. It's important to allow yourself some time to work through those changes and discover new possibilities in your connections to other people—whether they're new friends or old.

A word about romance

No matter what kinds of relationships you developed while abroad, it can be hard to leave good friends behind. But if there was somebody you became romantically attached to, leaving was no doubt painful. You may not know if or when you'll see your partner again, and even if you do, there are often huge hurdles to jump. You might come from different cultures, and be citizens of different countries, and at least one of you may have never seen where the other lives or met their friends or family in person. Students who do leave a romantic partner behind may feel very motivated to return to the host country—maybe even to look for a way to live there for a while.

On the other hand, if you left a romantic partner behind at home and are now returning to them, you may be experiencing very mixed feelings about being home. Many students find it difficult to return home to girlfriends or boyfriends because the closeness they expect to feel might not develop, at least not at first. The returnee has been away in another culture, their partner has been at home living their own life—they haven't shared face-to-face experiences in quite a while. For some people, this is a phase that eventually works itself out; for others, it can lead to a breakup, and if that happens, it is often one step in a process of greater change.

Many returnees who find themselves in difficult romantic transitions expect themselves to be able to "bounce back" into the relationship they had left behind months before. This expectation is often an unrealistic one: not only have you been living very different lives for the past months, but as we have seen throughout this book, your intercultural experience is likely to have caused you to question some of your beliefs, values, and likes and dislikes. Most returnees have changed in certain ways, and sometimes, those changes include feeling less connected to friends, romantic or otherwise.

If you are in a romantic relationship with somebody, either somebody from home whom you left to go abroad or from abroad whom you've left to come home, know that any difficulty you're experiencing is very normal. Transitions are difficult, and a transition within a close romantic relationship can be one of the most difficult. Be sure you are talking to trusted friends about your feelings, and continue to engage in the activities that are meaningful to you. If you're feeling especially sad or depressed, seek out a counselor in your university's counseling service or in your community.

Keeping connected

Often, the difficulty isn't so much in re-establishing old ties as it is in keeping new ones. If you made close friends overseas, you may feel some anxiety about whether or not you'll be able to stay in touch with them. And these fears aren't unreasonable: It can take a lot of work to maintain a long-distance relationship, romantic or otherwise. You might also feel that you aren't quite the same person you were abroad, and that as a result your friends from there won't connect as well with you anymore. Many times, students who study abroad feel that their "abroad" personalities were somehow different from their "home" personalities—that they were more outgoing while abroad, for example, or that they took more risks than they would back home. Of course, there is also the concern that you may not be able to visit again, will probably not communicate as frequently, and may, as a result, lose touch altogether.

While these concerns are certainly legitimate, there are steps you can take to help ensure that you do stay in touch if that's what you want. Connecting on social media, sending emails, texting, making the occasional phone call, using Skype, or even sending letters by post can help maintain connection. If you left friends behind in your host country with whom you want to maintain a relationship, don't be afraid to let them know. It's also important to recognize, though, that sometimes friendships do change and fade, for any number of reasons. For the ones that are important to you, do the work to keep them intact, but know that if they do fade, you have new experiences, and new relationships, on the horizon.

Take a minute to consider how you are keeping connected with friends from your time abroad:

- Who have you been keeping in touch with?
- Is there anybody you'd really like to keep up with who is not on that list? Why?
- What might you do to connect more with that person/those people?

- What is the nature of your communications with the people you are keeping in touch with? Mostly short and quick? More elaborated? What do you talk about?
- Is there anything about your communications you wish were different? For instance, would you like to talk via different media (e.g., email vs. Snapchat), or would you like to have more serious—or more lighthearted—exchanges?
- Is there any other change you'd like to make in your communications? If so, what steps could you take?

The traveler's club

Do you find that you spend a lot of time with other returnees now that you're home? Because renegotiating friendships can be a difficult process for returnees, many opt to spend time back at school or home mainly with other returnees. Students on campus, even those who have not studied abroad, have probably noticed them: groups of fourth-year students who hang out together in local cafés or the campus student center, talking about "last summer in Paris" or "my friends in Lusaka" or "the year I spent in Mexico City." These groups do serve the purpose of keeping returnees in touch with their overseas experiences, but sometimes, they can do more harm than good for their members.

While it's generally helpful to connect with others who share a reentering student's experience, staying isolated in the "returnee world" can prevent you from integrating your overseas experience into your everyday life at home. It also excludes others and can cause resentment and hurt feelings among your old friends. This does not mean that it's unhealthy to spend time with others who have also gone abroad—in fact, it can be quite useful in helping you make sense of your experience and adjust to life at home again—but if you find that you're hanging out exclusively with other returnees, you may want to look in other places for additional social contacts.

What does the research say?

First of all, the research tells us that—education-abroad or no education-abroad—friendships in the college years are important. The quality of peer relationships for college students has been shown in a number of studies to be a key factor in students' development during university.[5] Those peer relationships have been found to have an impact on everything from academic self-confidence and degree aspirations to drinking to fitness.[6] So it's not surprising that friendships play an important role in the education-abroad experience, too.

While there is limited research on the impact of education abroad on home-country relationships, there is an extensive literature on relationships students experience while abroad. In a study of international students in Hawaii, Blake Hendrickson and colleagues found that the more friendships an international student had with others from the host country, especially with a variety of people from the host country, the more content and less homesick they felt.[7] It can be difficult, though—as scholars Kazuhiro Kuro and Keith Simkin found in a study of Japanese students in Australia—to make strong connections with people from the host culture, since they have their own lives and preexisting connections.[8] In a large study of international university students across three regions of the US, scholar Elisabeth Gareis likewise found that more than a third of those students had no US friends, and that English-speaking and Northern or Central European students were more likely to feel satisfied with their friendships than were East Asian students. This suggests that the similarity between cultures plays a role in the ease with which cross-cultural friendships are formed. Often, students living abroad find it's easier to connect with other international students than to others from the host culture. Researcher Stephen Bochner and colleagues found, for instance, that students studying abroad in the UK were more likely to form friendships with other international students (not from their own country) than with British students.[9] And while friendships with host country others are important, it may be that having just a couple of strong relationships is more important than having a large number of relationships. In a study of international students in Nepal, researchers Colleen Ward and Arzu Rana-Deuba found that satisfaction with the quality, not quantity, of relationships with others was related to general feelings of contentment.[10]

When it comes to relationships in reentry, it will come as no surprise that the research suggests that relationships change when people come home from abroad. The patterns of change appear to depend on the type of relationship. In a study of American students who had been abroad, for instance, intercultural scholar Judith Martin found that while family relationships generally seemed to have changed in positive ways, friendship and romantic relationships had changed in ways that were more challenging to the student.[11]

Several studies suggest that the difficulty many returnees encounter in readjusting to relationships at home can contribute to more general feelings of dissatisfaction.[12] Interestingly, however, a study by researcher Sarah Brabant and colleagues found that students who felt they had adapted very well to life back home were more likely than others to have experienced changes in their relationships with friends from home.[13] This suggests that while experiencing relationship changes is often difficult, it can also be productive when those changes are linked to a sense of development.

The birthday party: Considering Lin-Lee's experience

Like Lin-Lee, in the vignette that began this chapter, perhaps you have experienced changes in your relationships since you came home. While abroad, students know that time at home does not stand still, but knowing that is one thing, and experiencing the reality of home after a long period away is another.

Lin-Lee knew that she had missed her cousin's wedding, but not being "in" on the jokes, having missed the experience, made her feel a little left out of the family circle, so important in collective cultures. Lin-Lee also knew her sister was older and would be more mature, but experiencing that maturity face-to-face was new.

Relationships, like that between Lin-Lee and her sister Tan, may need renegotiating in reentry. Spend some time reflecting on whether you have had to do any renegotiation of relationships since coming home. Lin-Lee had to realize, for example, that her sister now laid the table (a little thing really), but it used to be her job at home. Some relationships remain stable in reentry—like Lin-Lee's relationship with her grandmother. She remained her secret favorite grandchild and it showed in her grandmother's behavior, and was reassuring to Lin-Lee.

Often, time will help relationships sort themselves out into comfortable places once back home. Sometimes, relationships will end or fade when students return home. Remember the value of communication we discussed in the previous chapter? Clear, appropriate, thoughtful communication, directed at specific communication targets, at specific times, can help reestablish old relationships, end old relationships gracefully, and begin meaningful new ones.

Just as relationships may change, end, or need to be renegotiated by returnees, so do other kinds of changes occur for students in the reentry transition. In the next chapter, we will explore additional kinds of changes. These changes, and the realization by the returnees and those around them that they have changed, can bring both opportunities and challenges.

Notes

1 Muuss, R., Velder, E., & Porton, H. (1996). *Theories of Adolescence*. New York: McGraw-Hill.
2 Bureau of Labor Statistics, U.S. Department of Labor. *The Economics Daily*. Time spent in leisure activities in 2014, by gender, age, and educational attainment. Accessed July 30, 2017 at www.bls.gov/opub/ted/2015/time-spent-in-leisure-activities-in-2014-by-gender-age-and-educational-attainment.htm; Eurostat. Quality of life in Europe – facts and views – leisure and social relations. Accessed July 20, 2017 at http://ec.europa.eu/eurostat/statistics-explained/index.php/Quality_of_life_in_Europe_-_facts_and_views_-_leisure_and_social_relations
3 Perlman, D. & Fehr, B. (1986). Theories of friendship: The analysis of interpersonal attraction. In V.J. Derlega & B.A. Winstead (Eds.), *Friendship and social interaction* (pp. 9–40). New York: Springer.
4 McCabe, J. (2016). *Connecting in College: How Friendship Networks Matter for Academic and Social Success*. Chicago: The University of Chicago Press.
5 Astin, A.W. (1993). *What Matters in College? Four Critical Years Revisited*. San Francisco: Jossey-Bass; Pascarella, E.T. & Terenzini, P.T. (1991). *How College Affects Students*. San Francisco: Jossey-Bass.
6 Antonio, A.L. (2004). The influence of friendship groups on intellectual self-confidence and educational aspirations in college. *Journal of Higher Education*, 75(4), 446–471; Borsari, B. & Carey, K.B. (2001). Peer influences on college drinking: A review of the research. *Journal of Substance Abuse*, 13, 391–424; Carrell, S., Hoekstra, M., & West, J. (2011). Is poor

fitness contagious? Evidence from randomly assigned friends. *Journal of Public Economics*, *95*(7–8), 657–663.
7   Hendrickson, B., Rosen D., & Aune, R.K. (2011). An analysis of friendship networks, social connectedness, homesickness, and satisfaction levels of international students. *International Journal of Intercultural Relations*, *35*(3), 281–295.
8   Kudo, K. & Simkin, K.A. (2003). Intercultural friendship formation: The case of Japanese students at an Australian university. *Journal of Intercultural Studies*, *24*(2), 91–114.
9   Bochner, S., Hutnik, N., & Furnham, A. (1985). The friendship patterns of overseas and host students in an Oxford student residence. *The Journal of Social Psychology*, *125*(6), 689–694.
10 Ward, C. & Rana-Deuba, A. (2000). Home and host culture influences on sojourner adjustment. *International Journal of Intercultural Relations*, *24*, 291–306.
11 Martin, J.N. (1986). Communication in the intercultural reentry: Student sojourners' perception of change in reentry relationships. *International Journal of Intercultural Relations*, *10*, 1–22.
12 E.g., Gaw, K.F. (2000). Reverse culture shock in students returning from overseas. *International Journal of Intercultural Relations*, *24*, 83–104.
13 Brabant, S., Palmer, C.E., & Gramling, R. (1990). Returning home: An empirical investigation of cross-cultural re-entry. *International Journal of Intercultural Relations*, *14*(4), 387–404.

FOOD FOR THOUGHT

1. What are the pressures on relationships that can emerge in reentry? Be specific in your answer, using examples from the chapter to support your arguments. Which of those, if any, have you experienced, and how have you addressed (or could you address) them?
2. Is it important for a student coming home from studying abroad to spend time with other students who have also just come home from their time in a host culture? Are there any drawbacks to returnees spending time together? Clearly explain the reasoning for your answers.
3. What insight does Lin-Lee's reaction to the state of her relationships with her grandmother and her sister Tan give us into Lin-Lee's reentry experience thus far?
4. What three pieces of advice would you give to Mai (from Example Three in the chapter) as to how she might renegotiate her relationship with her parents? Be specific in your advice and provide clear reasoning to support that advice.

Suggestions for further reading

Beck, J. (2015, October 22). How friendships change in adulthood. *The Atlantic*. Accessed April 14, 2018 at www.theatlantic.com/health/archive/2015/10/how-friendships-change-over-time-in-adulthood/411466/

Demir, M. (Ed.). (2015). *Friendship and Happiness across the Life-span and Cultures*. New York: Springer.

Gareis, E. (2017). Intercultural friendships. *Oxford Research Encyclopedias: Communication*. Accessed April 14, 2018 at http://communication.oxfordre.com/view/10.1093/acrefore/9780190228613.001.0001/acrefore-9780190228613-e-161?rskey=Wr91lQ&result=4

Koschut, S. & Oelsner, A. (Eds.). (2014). *Friendship and International Relations*. London: Palgrave Macmillan.

Noller, P., Feeney, J., & Peterson, C. (2001). *Personal Relationships Across the Lifespan*. New York: Routledge.

8
WHAT'S NEW WITH YOU?

CHAPTER OVERVIEW

In this chapter, we'll explore some of the ways in which your perceptions, values, ways of thinking, and ways of interacting with the world around you have changed since your time abroad. We'll look at some developmental models that can help you make sense of changes you've noticed in yourself (and even some you may not have noticed yet)—and how these might benefit you in the future. We'll also take a look at a well-known model of intercultural competence, and you'll be able to consider how your own intercultural understanding has shifted.

Reentry fiction: You don't mean that!

"I think your dad is wrong," Ergun said calmly, seething with anger inside. The argument was becoming steadily more heated, and Ergun was glad that his coffee was finished so that he could soon make a graceful exit from the café. "You don't mean that!" exclaimed his friend Yamon. "She's his daughter, and he is just trying to protect her."

Ergun was learning that since he'd returned home to Turkey after his time in the Netherlands, he and his friends—who in the past agreed on everything—did not always see eye-to-eye. His friends' ideas now often seemed too rigid, too clear-cut. But, he kept trying to remind himself that he'd held similar ideas just twelve or so months before.

Yamon's sister, Hulya, wanted to go to college in the US, but their parents were concerned about her living so far away. His father was especially against the idea and did not feel it was appropriate for a young woman to live on her own in a foreign country. Hulya was angry, and, according to Yamon, was making life miserable for everyone in the family by persistently asking that she be allowed to go.

In response to Yamon's comment, Ergun mumbled "perhaps," and took his leave. Walking into the Istanbul sunshine, he looked around at the crowded sidewalks and listened to the traffic rushing by. He was eager to get home and check his messages as he'd left his phone by his bed. It was funny: before going to the Netherlands, he hadn't really been somebody who was always on a device. Now, he was almost never without one. He Skyped regularly with his Dutch friends and was grateful to be able to stay in touch so easily.

As Ergun sat on his bed and reached for his phone, he wondered whether Hulya would eventually be able to go to the US. She was smart and knew what she wanted to study. He felt sure that she would do well and have a great experience if she were allowed to go. But he knew Hulya's father well: a very traditional man who really loved and cared for his children, but who believed *he* knew what was best for them. Ergun pondered what kind of father he'd make… sometime *way* in the future.

Four new texts—yes! Ergun chuckled as he read his Dutch roommate Jaap's vivid description of his latest dating exploits. Ergun looked at the photo his friend had sent of the restaurant he'd been to last night, and remembered the place fondly: Ergun had eaten there many times himself. He'd found the Dutch dating scene very different from that in Turkey. Tracy, his British friend who'd also been studying in the Netherlands, had written a long and convoluted email about the trouble she was going through with her boyfriend. She was trying to decide whether to break up with him, take a break from him, or try and work through their problems. He could imagine her dramatically groaning and clutching her head in her hands as she struggled with what to do—she'd seemed very un-British to Ergun in the way she expressed herself.

"If I were Hulya's father, I'd let her go to the US," he thought to himself as he tapped out a quick reply to Jaap. But what if something bad happened to her while she was there—then how would he feel? Ergun still believed strongly in the importance of family, and of children's respect for their parents. But his views had shifted somewhat, and he felt more strongly now that children should have the freedom to make their own choices and mistakes. It was difficult for Ergun to reconcile these two strongly held views. As he walked to the kitchen to get a drink of water out the fridge, he decided he was glad that it was not up to him to have the final say about whether Hulya be allowed to go away to study or not.

REENTERING STUDENT QUOTES

- "While abroad, I recognized my strengths and worked harder on my weaknesses. I did things I might be hesitant to do here in the States."
- "I felt stronger and more confident in certain situations."
- "I've learned that there are few things that are fixed. My ideas of right and wrong have turned to various shades of grey."

> ➤ "I don't know how to get back to the person I was, or even if I know who she is anymore."
> ➤ "I feel more confident in myself."
> ➤ "I am much more direct with people."
> ➤ "I feel that I am less productive but more social."
> ➤ "My eating habits changed, the way I viewed alcohol changed, and the way I viewed transportation and city living definitely changed."
> ➤ "I take more risks and am genuinely happier."

Self-reflection

Are you the same person you were before you graduated from high school? Before you changed schools, moved to a new town, experienced a change in your family situation—or any other of the significant transitions of life? All of these kinds of experiences leave some indelible mark on us, and education abroad is no exception. Are you the same person you were before you left on your intercultural journey? In some ways, probably not. But it can take time and a lot of reflection to really understand how we have changed. As we saw in Chapter 3, actively reflecting on your experience can be a powerful tool in enriching your learning and personal development.

Take the time to explore—and to keep exploring—whether and how your values, beliefs, and interests have changed since you went abroad. While different people will experience different kinds and degrees of change, an intercultural living experience often impacts us in ways profound and subtle—sometimes so subtle that we realize only years later what those changes were. This can be awfully frustrating: a returnee may know they've changed, but they sometimes can't seem to articulate *how*.

How have you changed?

As a returnee, you need to take a while to consider how your thinking may have changed since you left to go abroad. A "before" and "after" comparison structure is a helpful way to begin this reflection process. For example, consider listing your leisure interests before and after your time abroad, examine whether your academic interests have changed or shifted at all, or whether and how the relationships and the things you value have changed before and after your time abroad.

Take a few minutes now to reflect. It may be helpful to write out your answers. You may not have answers to every question, and that's fine. Focus on the ones that feel relevant for you.

> *What do I spend time thinking about now that I did not think about before my experience abroad?*

What issues am I concerned or excited about now that I did not think about much before?

What do I seem to notice about my surroundings now that I did not notice before?

How do I interact differently with people now?

What features of my own personality, skills, talents, or areas for development am I aware of now that I was less aware of before?

How do I find myself disagreeing now with people whom I felt very much in sync with before?

What was I focused on, interested in, or worried about before that I no longer feel so concerned with?

For most returnees, the post-intercultural-experience list reflects a progression they've made during their time in the host culture and on their return home. And actually, this is the sort of progression that most college-age people go through; it's just that having an intercultural experience can hasten and intensify the process, and, sometimes, render it more profound and longer-lasting.

In 1970, a psychologist named William Perry[1] developed a model that helps explain the way this process works. This model is sometimes criticized for its origins within an "elite" group of subjects (Harvard University students, mostly male and white), and for its presumed assumption of the universality of that experience. However, we present it here because it is a seminal study that has spurred a number of well-researched similar models, and provides a useful structure for considering the ways in which we might change through an intercultural experience[2]. When we are young, and usually into our teens, Perry said, we tend to see the world in yes-or-no terms. Things are right or wrong, good or bad. When we encounter people with ideas different from the ones we've learned, we usually believe that they are wrong, or that they just haven't found the right information yet. We believe that every question has a "right" answer and that if we can find the right authority, we'll learn what that answer is.

When we get a bit older, according to Perry's model, usually in the traditionally mid-college years, we begin to see things less in black-and-white and more in shades of grey. We become more comfortable with feeling uncertain about the world around us, with not knowing exactly what the answers to all of our questions are. We are more and more able to think in abstraction, to think about "ways of thinking." And we often begin to feel that each person has a right to her or his own opinion.

By the time we reach the end of the college years, according to Perry, we see clearly that there are a multitude of ways to look at the world, and that each person has to decide on a particular lens through which to view the world. We are then able to choose one lens, or several lenses, for ourselves. For example, we may tend to look at things in terms of injustice and join causes that fight for equality. We may look for beauty in the world around us and seek out activities—such as creating art or designing landscapes—that help enhance that beauty. We may feel committed to a particular religious tradition, or to a particular political movement, or to a particular career field. Whatever "lenses" we use, we know that others may not use the same ones, and we feel comfortable with that difference.

Essentially, Perry's ideas are about becoming comfortable with ambiguity, diversity, and what can sometimes feel like chaos. Students returning from studying abroad have, in effect, had a crash-course in these subjects. For many, traveling internationally offers the first exposure to people who have beliefs, values, and norms of behavior that are fundamentally different from their own. Having to face these differences on a daily basis forces students to consider these deeply, to wrestle with them more directly and more fully than they probably ever have before.

Like Perry, Patricia King and Karen Kitchener developed a model in the 1980s[3] that helps us understand how people develop their ability to think reflectively—that is, to apply critical analysis to solving a problem while understanding that the answers may not be clear-cut—and this model can also help illuminate the education-abroad experience. As with the Perry model, it's important to note that the stages are not meant to box people in, since any individual might exhibit qualities of more two or more stages at once. They also may not apply equally well across all populations and subpopulations. But they offer a well-researched framework for understanding how people develop in their thinking about *how we know*.

King and Kitchener's model comprises seven stages, grouped into three broad periods:

1. **Pre-reflective thinking:** In this phase, people tend to take as "true" information that comes from authority, or from very concrete, observable evidence. There is not much grey area here: all propositions are seen as either true or false. People in this stage also tend to view all problems as if they have well-defined structure—and to ignore the messiness, ambiguity, and relativity inherent in many (if not most) real-life problems. A friend who tells you, "It's wrong to engage in illegal behavior; I don't care what your circumstances are," is probably engaging in pre-reflective reasoning. They are judging a behavior based on a predefined set of rules, with no questioning of those rules and no attempt to incorporate other information into their analysis.
2. **Quasi-reflective thinking:** In this phase, the individual has come to an understanding that knowledge implies uncertainty, but assumes that this uncertainty is due to lack of information. In other words—to put it simplistically—if only we had more information, we'd know the right answer. Quasi-reflective thinking can also be characterized by an oversubscription to the belief that all knowledge is relative: people in this phase might say that we can never really come to a conclusion, because we each see the truth from our own points of view. Imagine a friend says to you, "Women are treated differently in different cultures because those cultures hold different values and beliefs. I can't say their practices are good or bad; they're just different." You might argue that while cultural norms need to be considered in the conversation, we can still apply principles of human rights and feminist thought to an analysis of whether particular practices should be discouraged. Your friend is using

quasi-reflective thinking, and you are introducing reflective thinking—which we describe below.
3. **Reflective thinking:** If you're thinking reflectively, you know that problems are very often messy and complex, and that clear-cut solutions often are inadequate. People who use reflective thinking assume that knowledge is provisional—that there is always the possibility that our understandings will change—but are able to make judgments based on principles, information, and analysis. Reflective thinking acknowledges that knowledge is constructed by individuals, and allows for changing one's mind when new information or a new perspective warrants it. If your friend says, "I used to believe that prohibitions on drinking that exist in some cultures were completely misguided, but as I've read and talked to more people with experience in those places, I've come to understand other points of view," she is using reflective thinking in her exploration of the topic.

Take a few minutes to consider your own ways of thinking about knowledge. Be honest with yourself. Where do you tend to fall in terms of the stages Perry, or King and Kitchener describe? How have you changed over time? Since your experience abroad?

- When you were younger—say your grammar school or primary years—how might you have responded to questions of cultural, political, or social difference? It may help to think of a particular example. How would you have accounted for relativity in beliefs and values—or would you have done that at all? Would you have seen the question in clear-cut terms, or been aware of nuances? Would you have allowed for the possibility of changing your mind with new evidence?
- How might this have changed in your early teen years?
- How would you approach that issue now?
- In what ways do you think your education-abroad experience has played a role in any shift you've experienced around the way you think about knowledge?

If you're like most people, you probably find that you move back and forth a little among the categories in the models we presented earlier. Your level of knowledge on the topic, your level of interest, and even your mood can affect how you approach thinking through an issue or problem. But, on the whole, you probably find that your way of incorporating information, perspectives, and your own values into analyzing an issue has changed over the years. (And if you don't find that, chances are you don't recall how you thought about things as a younger person!) You probably will also find that your experience abroad plays a role in your approach to addressing complex issues, especially ones in which variation in world-view, values, or norms is central. This shift may become more apparent to you as more time passes since your experience abroad; sometimes it's hard to notice a change in yourself soon after the triggering event.

The differences each student studying abroad encountered will depend on the culture they visited and the people with whom they lived and interacted. In order to get a concrete sense of these differences, try to list the main differences you faced when abroad—the beliefs, practices, or ways of living that at first (and maybe always) seemed strange to them. A second useful reentry practice would be to separate out the items on that list with which you believe you eventually became more comfortable. Thinking about the process that led up to you feeling more accepting of these differences is critical. Did it happen easily, or did it take quite a while? Did the differences make you angry at first? How do you feel about them now? In trying to "sketch out" the process or stages you went through in moving from being annoyed or confused by cultural differences to becoming more comfortable with them, understanding of your experience (both abroad and in reentry) will grow.

The development in your thinking approach will serve you well, in ways far beyond studying (or working or living) abroad. In fact, the thinking skills you gained from your experience abroad will benefit you in whatever kind of work you do, wherever that might be. In 2009, Philip Gardner, Inge Steglitz, and Linda Gross[4] published a paper describing research they'd done on how college students present their international experiences to employers and how employers understand those experiences. They found that, by and large, students were not effectively explaining the relevance of their experiences abroad. They recommend that people who have had an education-abroad experience take some purposeful time to think through how they developed through the experience, and to develop ways of talking about that development that are relevant for the workplace—or whatever context they are moving into. For instance, students with experience abroad tend to gain comfort taking on projects that are unfamiliar (which requires comfort with ambiguity), are able to apply knowledge across contexts (which requires understanding of relativity), and finding novel solutions to problems (which requires seeing the problem in all of its complexity). Becoming a more reflective—and flexible—thinker benefits you *and* the people and organizations you're working with.

Gardner, Steglitz, and Gross recommend that after an education-abroad experience, individuals start by describing the key skills or competencies desired by employers, graduate schools, or others in the sector they would like to move into. The next step is to "unpack" your education-abroad experience and consider how it helped you develop the skills that will be appealing in your new sector. The authors suggest practicing first by doing this "unpacking" for a friend or classmate.

We'll take up this "unpacking" further later in the book. For now, though, consider the thinking and analysis skills you have developed through your international experience, and how those might map onto desired characteristics in your chosen field:

- What thinking qualities might your prospective employer/grad school/other entity value? Do they want people who can see various sides of an issue? Who are open to modifying their understanding of an issue based on new information? Who can balance information, values, and judgment?

- How do those qualities play out in the role you're hoping to have? Try to come up with some real-life scenarios of what they'd look like.
- What experiences did you have abroad that helped you develop these skills? How has your approach to thinking developed in a way that maps onto what your employer/grad school/other entity is looking for?
- How can you explain your new skills in a concise, compelling way?

We recommend thinking through these questions, and then practicing your explanations with a friend. Another great resource is your university or college's career center, or a career center in your community.

Moving toward intercultural understanding

As your thinking approach has morphed and developed, so has, no doubt, your understanding of intercultural difference. Intercultural communication theorist Milton Bennett offers a model that can be helpful as you think about this process of moving toward intercultural understanding.[5] Through his research, Bennett has found that people tend to go through six stages as they learn to operate in a truly intercultural frame of mind. Reentering students may see themselves and their experiences in Bennett's stages, or may find differences. Keeping in mind that it can take many, many years of intercultural immersion to reach the final stage is important, as most one-time study-abroad students *will not* have reached this stage. Remember also that Bennett does not suggest that students who have studied abroad should have reached the end of the process. We suggest you consider these stages as a tool to help you understand the process of becoming more interculturally sensitive. This model does *not* suggest that people should be divided into "good, culturally aware types" and "bad, ethnocentric types." Read through the stages below, and see if you can see any of yourself—or others you know—within them.

1. **Denial of difference:** People in this stage do not see substantial differences between cultures. They may tend to use "benign stereotypes," such as believing that people from a particular culture are "cute" or "quaint." There is generally no purposeful malevolence in this, but it does nothing to eliminate stereotypes or further intercultural understanding.
2. **Defense against difference:** Here, people begin to recognize differences, but with the view that their own ways are the best ways. They tend to use rigid categories for describing different groups. People in this stage may say things like "The French are so _____," or "Mexicans always _____."
3. **Minimization of difference:** In this stage, people begin to acknowledge superficial differences—in such areas as food and dress—among cultures, but not more profound differences. In stage three, we tend to say things like, "People are people," or "We're all the same deep inside."
4. **Acceptance of difference:** In stage four, we become culturally relativistic. People begin to judge and interpret behavior within its cultural context. We

move to a more profound understanding of culture, but may not feel comfortable engaging authentically within other cultural environments.
5. **Adaptation to difference:** People in stage five are able to operate equally well in two or more cultures. They can "switch cultural codes" the way a bilingual person can switch languages, becoming more effective intercultural communicators.
6. **Integration of difference:** In this final stage, the different perspectives of two or more cultures become a part of a person, so that they no longer have the feeling of "switching back and forth." Still, though, a person knows what their own, personal beliefs and values are, and they have no problem holding onto them regardless of the cultural context in which they find themselves. "Reality" is seen as a product constructed differently by different cultures, and people in this stage are able to judge for themselves which parts of those different realities make the most sense to them.

Many returnees can identify with aspects of several of the six stages, so you should not worry about trying to fit yourself neatly into one stage. The utility of Bennett's model, from our perspective, is that it provides returnees with another tool to make sense of their experiences in the host and home cultures.

Where do you think you fall in Bennett's model, and how has your experience abroad made an impact on your intercultural development? Recognizing that you may fall into more than one category, consider the following questions as you try to find yourself within the model:

- How do you react when you hear about unfamiliar, strange-seeming cultural practices? How did you used to react?
- To what extent do you tend to make blanket statements about particular groups, even silently to yourself? How does this compare to before your experience abroad? (Remember, it's common across humans to make generalizations—or to "essentialize" categories. It's how you process, critique, and make sense of those generalizations that matters.)[6]
- To what degree do you tend to underplay the more profound differences among cultures, and to focus mainly on the common facets of humans across cultures?
- How comfortable do you feel at this point "switching codes" culturally—taking off your Culture A hat and putting on your Culture B hat? (Note that even after an extended intercultural experience, many students do not feel fully comfortable with this.)

Wherever you are in the model—and recall that you may not fit neatly into one category—the best thing to do in order to further develop is to continue your exposure to intercultural situations. Equally important is to look for opportunities to process those exposures with people who can help you probe your experiences and your thinking, and explore your impressions and ideas. The more you continue to thoughtfully process your intercultural experiences, the more rich and complex your intercultural understanding will become.

What does the research say about how an experience abroad can change us?

Research findings on reentry suggest it is a major, multi-faceted experience.[7] Students in reentry are actually processing two experiences at the same time—their experience abroad and the transition to coming home—while at the same time trying to work out how they have changed, or even whether they have changed. Intercultural scholar Betina Szkudlarek notes that it's easy to assume that coming home is much easier than going away, and aptly suggests a "reality check" on this assumption: after time away, we have changed, and in our eyes, home has changed, too.[8] Home no longer looks the same after your perspective has been altered by an intercultural experience.

The literature also demonstrates that the impact of an education-abroad experience can show up in many areas of life. For instance, returnees may find they have a changed level of self and cultural awareness, are not associating with the same groups that they used to, have a new or tweaked set of values to live by, or are deciding to change vocational direction.[9] A study of Hong Kong Chinese university students with experiences abroad by Yang and colleagues found that students experienced three key areas of change: intercultural (for example, understanding another set of communication practices), personal (for instance, becoming more independent), and career-related (developing your analytical skills, for example).[10] You have likely seen similar changes in yourself.

A study by researchers Lorraine Brown and Iain Graham of international students in the UK had similar results, with students describing development in an array of realms, including feeling more confident about communicating interculturally, feeling more independent, having new views of home life, expanding or modifying their philosophies of life, and shifting their personal priorities. This rethinking of priorities, the researchers noted, revealed "the potential of the international sojourn to alter the future."[11] New priorities mean new interests, new activities, and possible new educational, personal, and professional avenues.

As you might imagine, increased intercultural understanding is an outcome commonly found in studies of the influence of education abroad on students, but its impact can depend on the goals you started out with. In a study of US college students, scholar Anastasia Kitsantas found that students who had made it a goal to improve their intercultural skills were more likely to actually increase those skills.[12] This doesn't mean that the rest of us didn't get anything out of the experience. It just means that you are more likely to make progress in areas that are important to you. You may have placed more emphasis on developing your communication skills, or on becoming more independent—both critical competencies for academic or professional success. And developing intercultural competence doesn't come only from education-abroad experiences. In her study of international students in the US, scholar Tracy Rundstrom Williams found that while education abroad had an impact on intercultural skills, simply engaging with other cultures in one's home country—for instance through intercultural friendships—enabled important gains in intercultural competence.[13]

Research also points to the significant impact of education abroad on students' career interests and choices. A large study by the US-based Institute for International Education of Students found that for most students, an education-abroad experience has a meaningful impact on career plans. This was especially (but not exclusively) the case for those who'd had more immersive experience, such as an internship or living with a host family.[14] The career-related impact of education abroad may not always be clear to the individual, though. As Norman Kauffmann and colleagues found, students often return from study abroad thinking that they want to do "something international," but are unsure what that might mean, exactly.[15] If that is the case for you, keep in mind that there are many ways to incorporate international content into a career—even if you live and work in your native country.

As students in reentry are working through the process of figuring out the changes that have taken place in them, their friends and family members can also be taken aback by changes in them, wondering what happened to the "old" person, and in some sense hoping that they'll get that person back. This idea is well illustrated in the words of a student who took part in a study by Norman Kauffmann and colleagues:

> My natural family wanted me to be the person I was before I left. They were not really accepting me as I was in the way I had changed… Yes I had, but that negative connotation was really a thorn in my side. I wished they could have celebrated the changes with me.[16]

Feeling you have changed when your environment has remained the same (and may even push back against your changes) can leave you feeling somewhat alone. In a study of US American students returning home after an experience abroad, researcher Kevin Gaw found that significant loneliness and isolation were experienced by about a third of returnees,[17] and other researchers have had similar findings, across countries and cultures. Feeling suddenly different at home is not easy. This means it's all the more important to connect with others who have had experiences similar to yours, and to seek support (from your university's study-abroad office, or an advisor or counselor) if you are feeling especially isolated.

While returning home as a changed person can be difficult, the benefits of that change usually outweigh the drawbacks—and as we've seen, the research bears this out. Whether it has become apparent to you yet or not, you have gained considerable perspective, insight, and skill as a result of your time abroad. You have yet to discover where those new attributes will take you.

You don't mean that: Considering Ergun's experience

Considering the student's experience that began this chapter, we realize that Ergun has changed, that he knows he has changed, and that part of that change came about from accepting, and then appreciating, a new set of cultural values and norms. He does not think it's fair that Hyula's father does not want her to go abroad for college. Ergun has come to accept a different set of values about family, parent-child relationships, and gender based on his experiences in the Netherlands. He feels pulled between traditional values of respect for elders and authority (represented by Yamon's father) and a newfound respect for gender equality and independence for young people. Luckily for Ergun, he is not the one having to make the decision about Hyula's academic future.

If you had to guess, which of Bennett's stages would you say Ergun was in? Most likely he is in the acceptance of difference stage, and might be stepping a toe into the adaptation to difference stage. It bears repeating that Bennett's model offers a framework for understanding intercultural development, and not a clear-cut separation of individuals into different categories. So Ergun is probably experiencing facets of two (or more) stages. Considering what experiences pushed you to develop your thinking and understanding of intercultural communication is important work to do. The reflection that takes place in reentry often helps makes those experiences clear. Such reflection becomes easier when you have useful ways to compare and contrast cultures. This will be the focus of the next chapter.

Notes

1 Perry, W. (1968). *Patterns of Development in Thought and Values of Students in a Liberal Arts College: A Validation of a Scheme.* Washington, DC: US Department of Health, Education, and Welfare.
2 Hofe, B. (2000). Dimensionality and disciplinary differences in personal epistemology. *Contemporary Educational Psychology, 25,* 378–405.
3 King, P. & Kitchener, K. (2004). Reflective judgment: Theory and research on the development of epistemic assumptions through adulthood. *Educational Psychologist, 39*(1), 5–18.
4 Gardner, P., Steglitz, I., & Gross, L. (2009). Translating study abroad experiences for workplace competencies. *Peer Review, 11*(4). Available at www.aacu.org/peerreview/2009/fall/gardner.
5 Bennett, M.J. (1993). Towards ethnorelativism: A developmental model of intercultural sensitivity (revised). In R.M. Paige (Ed.), *Education for the Intercultural Experience* (2nd edition, pp. 21–71). Yarmouth, ME: Intercultural Press.
6 Prentice, D. & Miller, D. (2007). Psychological essentialism of human categories. *Current Directions in Psychological Science, 16*(4), 202–206.
7 Sussman, N.M. (2000). The dynamic nature of cultural identity throughout cultural transitions: Why home is not so sweet. *Personality and Social Psychology, 4*(4), 355–373.
8 Szkudlarek, B. (2010). Reentry: A review of the literature. *International Journal of Intercultural Relations, 34,* 1–21. Quote p. 4.
9 Kauffmann, N., Martin, J.N., Weaver, H.D., & Weaver, J. (1992). *Students Abroad: Strangers at Home: Education for a Global Society.* Yarmouth, ME: Intercultural Press.
10 Yang, M., Webster, B., & Prosser, M. (2011). Travelling a thousand miles: Hong Kong Chinese students' study abroad experience. *International Journal of Intercultural Relations, 35,* 69–78.
11 Brown, L. & Graham, I. (2009). The discovery of the self through the academic sojourn. *Journal of the Society for Existential Analysis, 20*(1), 79–93. Quote p. 85.
12 Kitsantas, A. (2004). Studying abroad: The role of college students' goals on the development of cross-cultural skills and global understanding. *College Student Journal, 38,* 441–452.

13 Williams, T.R. (2005, Winter). Exploring the impact of study abroad on students' intercultural communication skills: Adaptability and sensitivity. *Journal of Studies in International Education*, 9(4), 356–371.
14 Norris, E.M. & Gillespie, J. (2009). How study abroad shapes global careers: Evidence from the United States. *Journal of Studies in International Education*, 13, 382–397.
15 Kauffmann et al. (1992). *Students Abroad: Strangers at Home – Education for a Global Society*. Yarmouth, ME: Intercultural Press. Quote p. 158.
16 Kauffman et al. (1992). Quote p. 116.
17 Gaw, K.F. (2000). Reverse culture shock in students returning from overseas. *International Journal of Intercultural Relations*, 24(1), 83–104.

FOOD FOR THOUGHT

1. Was Ergun's reaction to Hulya's situation an ethical one? Would you have done anything differently in his place? What, and why?
2. Are there limits to the idea of cultural relativity? At what point is it appropriate to make value judgments about the practices of another culture? Think of specific examples in your answer.
3. What are the experiences that push people forward in their approaches to thinking through issues and problems? How can that development be encouraged, and how is it sometimes held back?
4. In terms of the Bennett model, what are the approaches to portraying cultural difference typically used in the media—news, television, film? In what ways are these approaches useful, and in what ways counterproductive?

Suggestions for further reading

Bennett, M. (2013). *Basic Concepts of Intercultural Communication: Paradigms, Principles, and Practices*. Boston, MA: Intercultural Press.
Brookfield, S. (1991). *Developing Critical Thinkers: Challenging Adults to Explore Alternative Ways of Thinking and Acting*. San Francisco: Jossey-Bass.
Hogan-Garcia, M. (2007). *The Four Skills of Cultural Diversity Competence: A Process for Understanding and Practice*. 3rd ed. Belmont, CA: Thomson Brooks/Cole.
Shanghai International Studies University. Video on culture shock and encouraging your own personal development through an intercultural experience. Accessed April 14, 2018 at www.futurelearn.com/courses/intercultural-communication/0/steps/11084

9
A NEW VIEW OF HOME

> **CHAPTER OVERVIEW**
>
> *In this chapter, we'll consider how a student's home culture was seen in the host culture. In addition, we will discuss four different ways of explaining and exploring specific elements of culture. These dimensions of cultural variation will provide you with a frame to compare and contrast your home and host cultures. Making these comparisons will help you to make sense of your reentry experiences. We will also consider why giving our home culture a break is a good idea if we come home feeling hypercritical of the way things are done at home.*

Reentry fiction: It's not the same New Year

As the ATM spat out two twenty Canadian dollar notes (looking funny with the plastic-like see-through strip down their middle), Piper's mind wandered back to her time in Kenya, and she recalled the 1000 Kenyan shilling notes with the image of Jomo Kenyatta on them. She'd been back in Vancouver for several months now, having left Nairobi in time to be back home for New Year. Her semester at the University of Nairobi had been a rollercoaster.

Adimu, her best Kenyan friend, had admitted to Piper after they had become friends, that she thought Canadians and Americans were the basically the same. This had both surprised and bothered Piper who felt that Canadian and American cultures were different, and who wanted to be recognized as Canadian, not American, in Kenya. Piper had explained some of the differences to Adimu, like in governance, the bilingual system, and Canada's membership in the Commonwealth.

This discussion about Canada had prompted Adimu to tell Piper things about Kenya, and helped to develop the closeness of their friendship. Adimu explained that many Kenyan names had meanings that were important; for instance, her name meant *unique* or *rare* in Swahili. Adimu also helped Piper accept or at least understand parts of Kenyan culture that were different for her. She remembered how Adimu laughed at Piper's frustration that Kenyans often did not seem to be on time, and Adimu told her that people do not mind if someone does not turn up on the dot of an appointed meeting time. Piper would not miss that about Kenya now she was back in Canada. But, on the other hand, she would miss the ritual of greeting friends, of spending some time chatting with a friend or classmate you met on campus instead of rushing off with a quick "Hi, how're you doing?" to your next appointment.

As Piper zipped up her purse, having tucked her money safely away, she glanced at her watch, and saw that she only had five minutes to get from the student union to Professor Sawley's office. Dr. Sawley, Pam as she asked Piper to call her, was her senior honors thesis advisor. Piper really liked her and the mentoring relationship they had developed over the past three years. Professor Chelanga had been one lecturer in Kenya that Piper had not enjoyed studying with. He was very formal, which was OK, but not her preference, and called her Dawes or Miss Dawes, not Piper as she'd asked. His lectures were dull in Piper's opinion, and Adimu had told her that to get a good grade in his class, Piper should simply tell him what he wanted to hear on the tests and in class. Once she had tried to suggest a different interpretation of the novel they were studying from the one the professor had spoken about, and he marked her down. She never tried that again. Back home now, Piper appreciated Pam and her more laid back and interactive teaching style.

As she hurried down the brick path to Pam's office in the English department, Piper made a mental note to herself to send the birthday card to her Kenyan host family sister Bahati. She was turning seven in a few weeks' time, and Piper knew she would be thrilled to get a card in the mail from Canada. Piper had fond memories of her host family, and her time in Kenya had been enriched by spending time with them in their home over the course of the semester. Coming back to Canada in time for her family's annual New Year's Eve dinner had been important for Piper – it was a tradition she had loved ever since she could remember. Being with her mom, dad, and brother after not seeing them for several months while in Kenya was great. She had, however, had a few different moments during their celebrations when she wished more of her family had been gathered together. Whenever the Mwangis (her host family) had a celebration, their house would be full of aunts, uncles, cousins, grandparents, and neighbors. She loved that about Kenya. She missed that.

Pausing to catch her breath after climbing two flights of stairs, Piper walked toward Dr. Sawley's open office door. Pam heard her and glanced up, "Come on in Piper" she said, waving a hand to an empty chair. Focusing on the conversation to come, Piper mentally shook herself, and her Kenyan memories receded for the moment.

> **REENTERING STUDENT QUOTES**
>
> ➤ "I suddenly felt like America was the land of way-too-much."
> ➤ "Danes are very quiet and internal, whereas Italians are loud and expressive; it's important to realize the difference in our backgrounds…"
> ➤ "I was terrified of those huge, unpredictable American cities."
> ➤ "I long to have the lifestyle that is slower paced, like it was in my host country, where they took measures to promote family time and appreciate nature and art."
> ➤ "But I've come to realize that no matter how many rules we might have… we have a great amount of freedom that I did not find in Europe."
> ➤ "I try to notice little beautiful things. I have my coffee 'for here' when I can in little coffee shops. I go to Café Presse often. I actually even prepared myself for doing this in my journal while in Paris. I made a section of Parisian things to do in Seattle like see burlesque shows, go to French cafés, eat baguettes and cheese…"

How are we seen?

No matter whether you are an American or not, people in countries all around the world tend to have ideas about Americans and American cultures. Sometimes those ideas are rather strong. The point in using American culture here is simply to illustrate that people in a student's host culture, and no matter their national origin, would have some ideas about that student's culture. Perhaps they would have many ideas, perhaps they might express few; maybe their ideas would be accurate, or very inaccurate; they may be positive, or they could have negative ideas about a student's home culture and country.

When we're living as foreigners in another country, we are generally exposed to many different opinions about the host culture's views of different cultures. If an opinion is expressed about a visiting student's culture, often their initial reaction may be one of defensiveness; after all, who likes to be rigidly stereotyped and perhaps criticized? But with time, students usually come to see some truth in many of these stereotypes.

Can you recall people's views of your culture when you first arrived in your host culture to study abroad? Consider the following list of some of the most commonly heard characterizations of Americans by people in other cultures that we have gathered:

- Americans work too much; don't know how to relax
- Americans are extremely friendly; will talk to anybody
- Americans are informal even with strangers

- Americans are highly competitive and will try to achieve anything
- Americans lack a sense of identity
- Americans are naive and innocent
- Americans are not philosophical
- Americans love change
- Americans are obsessed with money
- Americans push themselves
- Americans are law-abiding
- Americans value freedom to such an extent that they are often not civil
- Americans have bad taste

We are sure that you could come up with a list of stereotypes that people in your host culture have of your culture. Take a few minutes to reflect on what people said to you about your home culture when you were abroad. Write down as many specific characterizations about your culture as you can, trying to recall specific instances where people in the host culture expressed ideas or opinions about your culture.

Now, spend some time considering whether you agree with each of the characterizations you've listed. Carefully consider why you do or do not agree with each characterization. Points of agreement or disagreement will highlight for you points of common and different understanding of home between you and your hosts.

Categorizing cultures

You probably had no trouble coming up with a long list of ways in which your host and home cultures differ. And, whether you're aware of it or not, doing this is an important step in the process of your reentry. Thinking through how, exactly, the host culture differed from your own culture can help you understand your own reactions and make sense of your experiences now that you're back home. This reflection process can also help you develop an even more sophisticated understanding of your home culture, which will be a set of insights you'll take with you wherever you go.

As you probably know, there are a number of different frames for looking at how cultures are different from or similar to one another. The utility of these frames are that they provide clear and specific ways for us to explain and describe elements of culture, and to then see how those frames influence communication, ways of doing and being. They allow us to compare cultures in specific ways. For you, they will allow comparison between your home and host culture. We will be looking at a set of frames that are known as dimensions of cultural variation.

First, let's consider some general concepts about dimensions of cultural variation. Each dimension should be thought of as existing on a continuum (or a line).

Different cultures fall somewhere between two hypothetical ends of that continuum, with the place a culture falls being the preference of the majority of people in that culture for that specific cultural element. Realize that the place a culture falls on a specific dimension of cultural variation may change over time, since cultures are not static. Realize, too, that there will be individuals in a culture or subgroups in a culture that do not hold the same preference as the majority on a specific dimension.

With that general understanding of these tools clear, we'll now look at four specific dimensions of cultural variation: high context vs. low context, monochronic vs. polychronic time orientation, individualism vs. collectivism, and high vs. low power distance. We think that these dimensions are ones that most of you will be able to relate to given both your experiences abroad and your experiences at home.

High context vs. low context

Developed by anthropologist Edward T. Hall, the labels *high context* and *low context* are commonly used to describe and compare cultures.[1] [2] Members of *high-context* cultures pay a great deal of attention to the *context* of a communication situation. Factors such as various specific elements of non-verbal communication being used in a communication interaction, status differences between those communicating, the time and location in which the communication is taking place, and the cultural cues that these all provide can carry more meaning than the words being uttered alone might. Verbal explicitness in communication is often seen as impolite. Members of high-context cultures may be better at reading "body language" than their low-context counterparts. In contrast, members of *low-context cultures* pay more attention to words themselves than to the context of the communication situation. Indirectness is seen as undesirable; people who do not speak explicitly are "beating around the bush." Nonverbal behavior is important but often plays a secondary role to verbal messages. Status differences may often be minimized in low-context cultures, and therefore, so are many of the implicit messages those differences might carry.

Upon understanding this dimension of cultural variation, you can now reflect on your experience and should now be able to mark an "X" where you think your home culture lies on this dimension's continuum, and an "O" where you think your host culture lies:

Low Context -- High Context

Consider, specifically, what characteristics of the culture made you place your X and O where you did, based on your own experiences in the host culture and at home. Doing this will be instructive, and can shed light both on cultural preferences with regard to high and low-context communication, but also on your own preference on this dimension. Do you still share your home culture's preference? Has your preference shifted at all? What are you most skilled at, high or low-context communication?

Monochronic vs. polychronic time orientation

Also first developed by Hall, this second dimension has to do with the way people view time.[3][4] In *monochronic* cultures, things are done one at a time. Your days are conceptualized as successions of separate activities: work, leisure, and home responsibilities. Time is viewed as a commodity, something you have and must make good use of by managing it wisely. This value can be seen in the way monochronic cultures talk about time as something that can be saved, wasted, bought, managed etc.

In *polychronic* cultures, by contrast, people feel very comfortable doing several things at once. The "flow" of the day is conceptualized as being more fluid and less scheduled. The "business" of the day can be put on hold if family or friendship responsibilities come up. Managing time is not as important as building relationships through it. Deadlines may be seen as flexible, and standards of punctuality differ in context.

You can now reflect on your experience abroad, and should be able to mark an "X" where you think your home culture lies on the continuum, and an "O" where you think your host culture lies:

Monochronic --- Polychronic

Do you still share your home culture's preference in terms of time? Has your preference shifted? Why do you value the time orientation you prefer?

Individualism vs. collectivism

This third dimension of cultural variation has been studied and applied to understanding culture and communication by a number of experts in the field, but it is probably known best as part of Geert Hofstede's model of cultural patterns.[5] This dimension has to do with the role of the individual in society. In *individualistic* cultures, the self is seen as existing distinct from the group. Each person is expected to be responsible for herself or himself. Individual rights are highly prized, and people are encouraged to improve their lives for themselves. Individualistic cultures tend to value competition, and individualistic cultures tend to foster creativity.

In *collectivist* cultures, on the other hand, the self is seen in relation to important groups, such as family. The individual's primary loyalty is to the group, and it is from the group that a person gets and maintains their identity. The good of the group is seen as more important than the rights of the individual, and in return for group loyalty, individuals can expect the group to look after their welfare. Cooperation and harmony are valued in collective cultures.

Now, mark "X" for your home culture and "O" for your host culture in terms of where you think they fall on this dimension of cultural variation:

Individualistic -- Collectivistic

Do you still share your home culture's preference around individualism or collectivism? Has your preference changed? Why do you think you value the orientation you prefer?

High vs. low power distance

Also developed by Hofstede, this fourth dimension addresses interaction between people with different statuses.[6] In *low power distance* cultures, status differences are minimized and often not outwardly apparent in people's interactions. Equality is seen as an ideal. Formal or honorific titles such as "Dr." or "Professor" are used sparingly, and even people from different social classes will tend to interact informally. People in authority positions (such as teachers, parents, and supervisors) are commonly challenged by those they lead, and in many cases such challenge is even encouraged. In *high power distance* cultures, however, status differences are given much attention. People tend to believe that each person holds a certain status, and status differences are not seen as a negative thing. Honorific titles are commonly used, and people with different levels of authority interact with a high degree of formality. People in positions of authority are rarely questioned.

Where do you think your home culture lies on this dimension, and your host culture? Mark an "X" for your home culture and a "O" for your host culture:

High Power Distance -------------------------------- Low Power Distance

Have your preferences and values shifted at all here? Why do you think you prefer one orientation over another?

How far apart are your home and host cultures on these four dimensions of cultural variation? Had you thought about these specific differences before reading this chapter? If so, did you have a label to categorize these differences and help you understand them?

For many returnees these kinds of differences, highlighted by the four dimensions we have just discussed, are precisely what moves them to begin questioning the values and assumptions they grew up with. By doing exercises such as the ones above, you will be able to do things like identify aspects of the host culture that you miss, and think about how you can make them a part of your life here at home. If you enjoyed a more fluid sense of time in the host culture, you could take steps to "decompartmentalize" your everyday life back home, perhaps by changing your schedule. If you miss a more collectivist orientation than you have at home, there may be something you can do to bring that value back into your life, such as volunteering in the community.

While you won't be able to replicate the way of life you might have enjoyed during your intercultural experience (nor should you necessarily try to do this), you *can* change things about your own life to better match your personal tastes and values, to suit elements of your new identity.

Giving your home culture a break

Being a returnee provides a special outlook on a home culture: for perhaps the first time in your life, you are able to view it from an outsider's perspective, and that is an opportunity many people may never have. But along with this expanded perspective can come a new kind of one-sidedness. For example, often, recent American returnees are hypercritical of US culture: they see all that is wrong and little that is right. They frequently compare the US to the host country, with the US almost always on the losing side. And with all this complaining, they can begin to fray the nerves of their friends and family members. And students who study in host cultures with well-developed communication and technological infrastructure might feel hypercritical when they return home and find Internet access difficult to obtain and much more expensive than in their host culture.

It can sometimes be difficult *not* to be hypercritical, especially when you have just given up ways of living that felt new and good and exciting to you. At the same time, returnees often find they have a new sense of appreciation for their home cultures. For example, many American returnees complain about what they see as the rampant materialism they see in the US but, at the same time, express pleasure in having the freedom to choose whatever product suits them best.

If you find yourself having negative feelings about your home culture, it is a good practice to make a list of the things that have bothered you since coming home, and then to balance that list off with a list of the things for which you have found a new appreciation back home. Write down five things that bug you about home, and then five things for which you are grateful or appreciate more about home than you did before you studied abroad.

If you find that in reentry you are tending to be mainly critical of your home culture, it is important to try to reach a balance in your point of view. Reminding yourself of the things you may have missed while you were abroad, and of the things you're glad to have once again, is a positive step. But don't push yourself too hard. For many returnees, a period marked by some negative feelings about the home culture is an important part of the transition process.

104 A new view of home

What does the research say?

It has been found that one of the themes in intercultural reentry is people often compare their home and host cultures. As one returnee interviewed by Victoria Christofi and Charles Thompson put it, "Knowing two countries is difficult because you are always comparing the two."[7] Lorraine Brown and Iain Graham found returnees reported being aware that "realigning students' new self with the home culture might be problematic."[8] Research suggests that students in reentry may also feel a certain amount of ambivalence toward their home culture.[9] Victoria Christofi and Charles Thompson's work suggests that returnees may have a new view of home that challenges their idealized version of home that they had in mind when they were abroad.

Ahn Le and Barbara LaCost's[10] work with returning Vietnamese students who had studied in the US confirms that in the shock phase of reentry, a view of home that is consistent with a different world-view that may be critical of the home culture can be seen. For example, one respondent reported getting upset about people in Vietnam running red traffic lights, not putting on their seatbelts when driving cars, and littering on the streets. Another example of research highlighting some practical disappointments given a new comparative view of home upon reentry include New Zealand returnees not liking the cost of living back home as compared to in the European Union, with New Zealand having higher tax rates, higher food costs, and higher prices to buy a house than in returnees' host cultures.[11]

Yuliya Kartoshkina's[12] study found that students returning to the US after studying abroad indicate a new awareness about home in reentry. Their language used in some of their answers indicates this, with students starting sentences with phrases like "I became more aware…" or "I realized…" or "I noticed…" The kinds of realizations these students had about home in the US included the fast pace of life in that culture, the food (perceived as not too healthy in the main), and the benefits of being able to own and drive their own car. Students also reported being more critical of the political system in the US and the general American lifestyle, while they appreciated the education system and how efficient and organized American society could be (as compared to their host countries).

This new awareness of home and home culture was also found in another study of Chinese students who returned to China after studying in the UK.[13] Seventy-five percent of the Chinese returnees in this study by Qing Gu and Michele Schwiesfurth believed they were more knowledgeable about their home culture and Chinese background than people who had not spent time abroad as they had. Students also reported gaining a clearer sense of what China's place in the wider world was after they had their education-abroad experiences.

Fiction story: Considering Piper's experience

In the story that began this chapter, Piper came back from Kenya to Canada in time for New Year's Eve; she wanted to be with her family for that celebration.

Though she enjoyed being back and with her immediate family, she also thought about the time she spent during celebrations with her Kenyan family, and realized she enjoyed having all the Mwangis' extended family always involved too. Having her own and host family experiences to compare offered Piper a new view of the way Canadian culture contrasted with Kenyan collective culture manifested in celebration rituals.

She came to have an appreciation for Canadian culture being more monochronic, when faced with the more polychronic Kenyan culture. She liked punctuality. However, she valued the time people took to greet each other and chat for a while on campus, an element of cultural practice in Kenya related to having a more polychronic time orientation.

Further, Piper did not really enjoy the higher power distance culture in Kenya manifested in the interaction between her professor and herself. She did not prefer the formality, the teaching style with all authority invested in the professor she'd experienced in Kenya. She much preferred the lower power distance relationship she had with her Canadian professor and mentor.

Hopefully, in Piper's experiences, you can see how using the four dimensions of cultural variation discussed above, as tools for reflecting on your own experience, will be helpful to understanding and managing reentry. You may be able to see your own culture in a new light when compared to the host culture along these dimensions. You may also be able to explain things that you liked or did not like in the host culture with more specificity now that you understand these dimensions of cultural difference.

Perhaps looking up some other ways in which we can explain and describe culture will aid you in coming to new and clearer realizations about home and host cultures in reentry. What may also help you be proactive in reentry are the ideas about having a global perspective that we discuss in the next chapter of the book.

Notes

1. Hall, E.T. (1973). *The Silent Language*. New York: Anchor Books.
2. Hall, E.T. (1977). *Beyond Culture*. New York: Anchor Books.
3. Hall (1973).
4. Hall (1977).
5. Hofstede, G. (1977). *Cultures and Organizations: Software of the Mind*. New York: McGraw-Hill.
6. Hofstede (1977).
7. Christofi, V. & Thompson, C.L. (2007). You cannot go home again: A phenomenological investigation of returning to the sojourn country after studying abroad. *Journal of Counseling & Development, 85*, 53–63. Quote p. 57.
8. Brown, L. & Graham, I. (2009). The discovery of the self through the academic sojourn. *Journal of the Society for Existential Analysis, 20*, 79–93. Quote p. 89.
9. Steyn, M.E. & Grant, T. (2007). "A real bag of mixed emotions": Re-entry experiences of South African exiles. *International Journal of Intercultural Relations, 31*(3), 363–389.
10. Le, A.T. & LaCost, B.Y. (2017). Vietnamese graduate international student repatriates: Reverse adjustment. *Journal of International Students, 7*(3), 449–466.

11 Chaban, N., Williams, A., Holland, M., Boyce, V., & Warner, F. (2011). Crossing-cultures: Analysing the experiences of NZ returnees from the EU (UK vs. Non-UK). *International Journal of Intercultural Relations, 35*, 776–790.
12 Kartoshkina, Y. (2015). Bittersweet reentry after studying abroad. *International Journal of Intercultural Relations, 44*, 35–45.
13 Gu, Q. & Schweisfurth, M. (2015). Transnational connections, competences and identities: Experiences of Chinese international students after their return 'home'. *British Educational Research Journal, 41*(6), 947–970.

FOOD FOR THOUGHT

1. Which of the four dimensions of cultural variation discussed in this chapter had the most influence on your experience abroad? Why?
2. If a student returns to a high power distance culture after having studied and adjusted to a very low power distance culture, what are some specific elements of power distance they might have to readjust to in the classroom context back home?
3. Why is it important for a student in reentry to give their home culture a break at times during their transition home?

Suggestions for further reading

Gu, Q. & Schweisfurth, M. (2015). Transnational connections, competences and identities: Experiences of Chinese international students after their return 'home'. *British Educational Research Journal, 41*(6), 947–970.
Le, A.T. & LaCost, B.Y. (2017). Vietnamese graduate international student repatriates: Reverse adjustment. *Journal of International Students, 7*(3), 449–466.
The Reluctant Girl Scout blog. *Return with an Itch.* September 15, 2013. Accessed December 15, 2017 at https://thereluctantgirlscout.com/2013/09/15/return-with-an-itch/

10
AN EMERGING GLOBAL PERSPECTIVE

CHAPTER OVERVIEW

In this chapter, we'll explore how your education-abroad experience has influenced the way you think about your place in the world and about what is happening beyond your doorstep. We'll look at some models that can help you situate your own development in this area, and consider how to take steps to continue becoming more globally aware and engaged.

Reentry fiction: On the streetcar

Shane was out of breath as he boarded the streetcar, already running late to meet friends for dinner. It had been nearly a month since he'd been back in Toronto, and he'd seen friends only a handful of times. He'd been so busy organizing himself for his last year at university—sorting out a place to live, and working out some class registration snags—that he'd hardly had time to have fun. Taking his seat, he caught sight of a woman reading a newspaper in Spanish, and his mind went to the media course he'd taken while in Salamanca. Learning about the Spanish media system, and especially the paper he'd written on media coverage of political campaigns, gave him a new perspective on politics. He had always been a "political person," but that course led him to realize that his understanding of politics was far less broad than he'd always assumed. He had a strong grasp of the intricacies of the Canadian political system, and the US system to some degree, but—if he was being honest with himself—he had never really thought about systems in other parts of the world. Focusing on the Spanish context gave him insight into the issues the Spanish people cared and fought about. While many of those issues were also familiar at home—education, the economy, immigration—the particularities were different, and in studying them he felt both a closer connection to the people he was meeting in Spain and a greater appreciation for the challenges, big and small, they faced.

Shane remembered having a conversation with Belén, his roommate's girlfriend, about the difficult economic situation her family was in, and sensing the deep frustration she felt about the nation's economic troubles. He also remembered having a conversation with the housekeeper of a friend's family, a middle-aged woman named Luz, who had come to Spain from Ecuador to find work. Luz told Shane that several of her friends in similar situations had returned home, unable to find lasting employment. Shane remembered feeling surprised, because he had never thought much about immigration and economic issues outside of North America—and afterwards feeling embarrassed that he had been so provincial in his thinking.

As he rang the bell for his stop, Shane thought about what his friends would be talking about at the restaurant, and wondered if telling stories about Spain would bore them. It might, he decided, and committed to restraining himself from focusing on his trip abroad during the meal.

> **RETURNING STUDENT QUOTES**
>
> - "I realize how small my little part of the world is now."
> - "I feel like I want to be more engaged in international issues. I don't want to care just about what's happening in my own town."
> - "When I talk to my friends from home, they don't seem to really care what's happening in other parts of the world. I think it really matters—we're all connected."
> - "Reading the news now, I just naturally drift to what is happening in China. I feel like I need to stay informed so that I can help inform other people."
> - "I have friends in South America now, so it matters to me what is happening there."
> - "It's more important to me now to connect to other kinds of people, in other places. I don't want to just always be with people like me."

Spending time in a different country has a way of bursting our individualistic bubbles, of bringing to the center of our awareness the fact that our experience is just one tiny sliver of the range of human experience on the planet. Of course, this "bursting" effect varies greatly by individual, but you probably have encountered some degree of awakening to the broader world through your time abroad. If you had previously lived in one place for all or most of your life, and hadn't been engaged in international studies or issues, that awakening was probably more dramatic; if you already had some experience with other parts of the world, your awakening may have been more subtle. But you no doubt feel in some way more connected to another part of the world than you did before.

What does it mean to have a "global mindset"?

The terms *global engagement* and *global mindset* get tossed around a lot, but it's not always clear what, exactly, we mean when we use them. What does it mean to be thinking globally?

One answer to this question comes from researchers Duarte Morais and Anthony Ogden,[1] who developed a research-based inventory for global citizenship, which could be used to assess the impact of an education-abroad experience. The model they use comprises three core features. Read about those features below, and consider how you would rate yourself at this point on each one, in terms of how much it describes you. Use a 1–5 rating scale, with 1 being low and 5 being high:

1. **Global competence.** Global competence is made up of three components:
   a. Self-awareness, or confidence that you can make a difference globally.
   b. Intercultural communication, or skill in communicating with people from other cultures.
   c. Global knowledge, or feeling confident in your understanding of global issues.
2. **Global civic engagement.** Global civic engagement is also made up of three components:
   a. Involvement in civic organizations, or taking part in organized activities to benefit global causes.
   b. Having a political voice, or making your opinions heard through emails, letters, protests, and so on.
   c. Global civic activism, for example, avoiding the purchase of goods or services that exploit international resources or individuals.
3. **Social responsibility,** or the belief that there should be more equality in the way resources are distributed among people around the world.

How did you rate yourself? Were there any surprises? Were you fairly consistent across the board, or were there some low and some high areas? Keep in mind that having a "low rating" in any given area does not mean you are not globally engaged; it simply means that this area is not something that is at the fore for you, at least for the moment. You might be more interested in engaging in intercultural activities than in taking political action, or vice versa. Or you might be passionate about buying fair-trade goods, but not spend much time thinking about making your voice heard in other ways.

Rather than using this model as a way to rate yourself, make use of it as a gauge for where your current interests lie, and where you might like to develop. For instance, have you thought about being more politically engaged around global issues, but not known where to start? Take this as an opportunity to do some research about organizations at your university or in your community that you could take part in. Or, have you wanted to improve your ability to communicate effectively with people from other cultures but haven't made progress yet? Consider taking an intercultural communication class, or joining a "buddy" program with your university's international office.

However much progress you feel you have yet to make in being globally engaged, you are probably further ahead than many because of your experience abroad, and your interest in learning about another culture or cultures. You may have found that your friends and acquaintances from home don't share your global perspective, and as a result you may at times feel frustrated in conversations about global or intercultural issues. Consider the following scenario:

> *Terrance, who spent the last year studying and traveling in Latin America, is back home in Chicago and hanging out with friends at a café. The topic of immigration comes up, and a lively conversation ensues. A couple of people mention friends they have whose parents are undocumented (are in the country without legal status). This leads to discussion of whether the nation's immigration laws need to be changed, and one person makes a comment about Mexicans "going back where they came from." This startles Terrance, and he suddenly feels his face get hot. He confronts the person who made the comment, voices rise and tempers flare, and soon the whole group is arguing, loudly. Terrance is exasperated, and after a few minutes he simply stands up and leaves.*

Have you encountered a situation similar to Terrance's? How have you handled it? These encounters are difficult, and it's easy for frustration to escalate to anger. If you find yourself strongly disagreeing with somebody on a global or cross-cultural issue, keep the following things in mind:

- **Know what you want to say.** If you have strong views on particular issues (such as immigration), inform yourself and stay up-to-date on the issues, so that you'll feel confident explaining your position and offering a rationale.
- **Avoid the urge to trip people up.** When we have strong feelings on an issue, it's easy to fall into the trap of wanting to catch our "opponents" in faulty logic, or otherwise demonstrate that their arguments are without reason. This usually backfires, because it causes even stronger feelings of anger and resentment in the other party. Stay focused on what you believe and want to communicate, and where you might be able to find points of agreement, rather than on what the other person is doing wrong.
- **Remember that people bring their own life experiences to the table.** Your beliefs and values are informed by a lifetime of experiences, and so are the other person's. If you don't understand why somebody holds the views they do, try to learn more about them. Ask questions, like "That's interesting, and not the way I see it. I'm interested to hear why you see it that way." If you can better understand the experiences that have shaped their perspectives, chances are you'll have a more productive conversation.
- **Look for underlying common beliefs.** Often, when we disagree about an issue, we're so focused on that particular issue that we don't take time to

explore underlying beliefs or goals. In your conversation, ask yourself: Is there anything we agree on? You might even ask this question out loud. For instance, perhaps you and a conversation partner have different beliefs about people's rights to observe religious practices without any constraints. It may be that a goal you have in common is freedom from discrimination, but you have differing ideas about how best to achieve that. Try to get to those underlying common goals by remaining open and curious, asking why, and being willing to explore your own deeply held fundamental beliefs.
- **Keep it in perspective.** These issues are all important, but they're large, complex ones that won't go away anytime soon. You and your friend will not solve them by duking it out one afternoon in a café. When things get tense, remind yourself that you are part of a much larger conversation, and that there are probably many other issues on which you and your friend can agree. Take a breath, and move forward.

Another way to answer the "What is a global mindset" question focuses on the world of work. It won't surprise you that organizations of all types increasingly value international experience and global-mindedness in their employees, and there is great interest in the world of management and leadership in better understanding what global qualities are most important, and who is most likely to bring them. Many students who study abroad are interested in international careers,[2] but even if you are not, the global perspective you bring is valuable to an organization. International management scholars Mansour Javidan and Mary Teagarden[3] developed another research-based model for describing the components of a global mindset in the business world. The model has three components:

1. **Intellectual capital,** including deep knowledge of international business (or related field), an ability to think through complicated problems, and a way of thinking that takes global issues and interests into account.
2. **Psychological capital,** including a commitment to cultural diversity, a drive to have new experiences, and a confidence in engaging in global situations.
3. **Social capital,** including an ability to put yourself in somebody else's shoes and an ability to act diplomatically.

Regardless of whether you've got your sights set on a career in international business, this model can be useful in helping you think about the attributes that you can offer to any sort of organization. Take a few minutes now to jot down some notes on the qualities you have to offer that fit more or less into these categories. As you write, think in terms of the type of organization you might like to be a part of, whether that's a business, an educational institution, a volunteer organization, a service organization, a graduate or professional school—or something else.

- What kinds of intellectual capital would you bring? What ways of thinking have you developed—either through your education-abroad experience or

elsewhere—that will help you solve problems? What knowledge have you gained about interacting with other cultures that will enable you to develop productive relationships?
- What kinds of psychological capital will you bring? How could your commitment to globalism or diversity benefit an organization? How does the drive to have new experiences which you demonstrated in your journey abroad translate to the impact you could make in an organization? What kinds of confidence have you gained from being abroad (or otherwise) that would offer a benefit?
- And finally, what kinds of social capital would you bring? How have you learned through your experience abroad to more easily put yourself in somebody else's shoes, to understand where they are coming from, what their intentions are—even when they may not be communicating those things directly? How have you learned to be diplomatic, to negotiate differences in a way that allows people coming from different perspectives to feel they are being heard and getting something that is valuable to them?

Thinking through and answering these questions will not only help you better understand your own skill set; it will also provide you with a ready-made "elevator speech" to help explain how your overseas experience has helped prepare you for being a productive member of the organization of your choice.

Beyond the global dimension, an experience abroad can put you in a great position to become more sensitive to the cultural, ethnic, racial, and other differences that exist in your home country. Consider how you generally think about the diverse array of people within your home culture, and how their experiences may differ from your own. These might be people who have a different ethnic or racial identity from yours, a different religious outlook, a different gender or gender identity, a different sexual orientation, or different political ideas. Many people—probably most people—find it challenging to engage effectively across many of these lines of difference. As we grow, learn more about the world, and have new life experiences, though, our attitudes toward and approach to diversity can change, sometimes dramatically.

For each of the following categories, rate how much you feel you have changed over time, with 1 being none and 5 being very much:

- My curiosity about other cultures or ways of life
- The speed with which I make assumptions about people without learning something about them first
- The degree of irritation or frustration I feel with people who have ways of life different from my own
- My ability to look for the individual person beneath the exterior
- My belief that I can learn things from people who are different from me
- My interest in the music, food, literature, film, etc. of cultures or groups different from my own

- My willingness to put myself in situations where I might be the only person from my cultural or ethnic group

How did you rate yourself? If you feel that you have not changed considerably, it may be that you are experiencing change slowly, and/or that you simply are not aware of a change in yourself. It can sometimes take years to see clearly how one has changed over time. Reflecting on it can help raise your awareness, though, and make it more likely that you'll continue to develop and expand your perspective.

What does the research say about education abroad and global engagement?

A number of studies have examined the impact of education abroad on people's views toward global issues. Researchers Bernhard Streitwieser and Gregory Light argue that studying abroad does not automatically make for a "global citizen," and examined the various ways in which students returning from an experience abroad understand the notion of global citizenship. They found that students held beliefs along a continuum, identifying five distinct notions: (1) that we are all global citizens by default, by virtue of living on the globe, (2) that we are global citizens if we have global ties (e.g., family), (3) that we are global citizens if we think beyond our borders, (4) that we are global citizens if we engage actively with other national or cultural communities, and (5) that we are global citizens if we feel and act on a responsibility to improve the world both within and beyond our own borders.[4] Wherever you might place yourself among these categories (and that might be in more than one category), you can continue to think about what "global citizenship" means to you, and how you would like to enact it in your own life.

In another study, Kevin Kehl and Jason Morris found that university students who completed a semester-long education-abroad program were more globally minded than both students who had been abroad for a short time *and* students who *intended* to study abroad for a full semester. The researchers assessed global-mindedness using a survey instrument that measures qualities including sense of responsibility for the world beyond you, appreciation for cultural diversity, a sense of interconnectedness, and a belief that you can make a difference globally.[5] While returnees were surveyed only at the end of their programs, the fact that semester program returnees were more globally minded than both short-termers and pre-departure students suggests that length of stay may impact development of global mindedness[6], and the idea that longer programs make a greater impact is supported by other studies.[7] It's important to note, though, that a number of studies document the important gains for students on short-term education-abroad programs, as well.

Other researchers have looked at the impact of education abroad on people's attitudes toward diversity more generally. Using longitudinal data from a US national study, and controlling for selection bias (in other words, for the possibility that people who study abroad are already more predisposed to all things intercultural), education researchers Mark Salisbury, Brian An, and Ernest Pascarella found that while an education-abroad experience did not necessarily bring heightened levels of sensitivity to diversity, it did increase college students' level of interest in engaging with diverse others.[8] This in itself is an important stepping-stone to continuing a lifelong study—formal or informal—of intercultural issues and developing a wide range of intercultural skills.

On the streetcar: Considering Shane's experience

Looking back at Shane and his return home from Spain, it's clear that he has become more globally engaged as a result of his abroad experience. He feels a stronger sense of global citizenship, a greater sense of caring, and even responsibility, for the welfare of people outside of his own community. Although he hasn't yet taken direct action with it, he has a stronger sense of social responsibility than he's had before. He isn't sure if his friends will have the same perspective, and he's not quite sure how to navigate that difference. He may feel like more of a global citizen than he has in the past, because he thinks beyond his borders, and he feels a responsibility to help improve things for people in other parts of the world. Whether and how he does take action toward those goals remains to be seen, but chances are he will, even if only in local ways.

Shane's experience is not uncommon among students who have education-abroad experiences: being abroad can open our eyes to certain injustices that we have not had to think about before. It can also give us empathy for people whom we may simply not have understood well before. The task before Shane, and before you if you find yourself in a similar situation, is to figure out how to take that interest and energy and turn it into action.

In the next chapter, we'll turn to the question of moving forward after your experience abroad, considering what kinds of action you may want to take as an extension of that experience. We'll consider more fully the ways in which you can continue to develop not just intercultural skills, but a wide range of skills and abilities. We'll also delve further into linking your experience abroad to your future educational and career plans, including how you can most effectively talk about your experience abroad with prospective employers.

Notes

1 Morais, D. & Ogden, A. (2011). Initial development and validation of the global citizenship scale. *Journal of Studies in International Education, 15*(5), 445–466.
2 Mohajeri Norris, E. & Gillespie, J. (2009). How study abroad shapes global careers: Evidence from the United States. *Journal of Studies in International Education, 13*(3), 382–397.
3 Javidan, M. & Teagarden, M. (2011). Conceptualizing and measuring global mindset. In W.H. Mobley, M. Li, & Y. Wang (Eds.), *Advances in Global Leadership (Advances in Global Leadership, Volume 6)* (pp. 13–39). Bingley, UK: Emerald Group Publishing Limited.
4 Streitwieser, B. & Light, G. (2016). The grand promise of global citizenship through study abroad: The student view. In E. Jones, R. Coelen, R. Beelen, & H. de Wit (Eds.), *Global*

and Local Internationalization: A Crucial Nexus (pp. 67–73). Series editor: Philip Altbach. Rotterdam. Sense Publishers.

5 Hett, J.E. (1993). *The development of an instrument to measure global-mindedness.* Doctoral dissertation, University of San Diego. *Dissertation Abstracts International, 54*(10), 3724A.

6 Kehl, K. & Morris, J. (2007). Differences in global-mindedness between short-term and semester-long study abroad participants at selected private universities. *Frontiers: The Interdisciplinary Journal of Study Abroad, 15,* 67–79.

7 Dwyer, M.M. (2004). More is better: The impact of study abroad program duration. *Frontiers: The Interdisciplinary Journal of Study Abroad, 10,* 151–163.

8 Salisbury, M., An, B., & Pascarella, E. (2013). The effect of study abroad on intercultural competence among undergraduate college students. *Journal of Student Affairs Research and Practice, 50*(1), 1–20.

FOOD FOR THOUGHT

1. What are the barriers to developing a "global mindset"? Think about emotional and cognitive barriers, institutional barriers, and cultural and political barriers. How can we navigate around those barriers?
2. What are the concrete things you can do now to become more engaged globally? What will it take for you to do those things?
3. What is the difference between having a global mindset and being interculturally competent? Can a person have one and not the other?

Suggestions for further reading

Acaro, T. & Haskell, R. (Eds.). (2009). *Understanding the Global Experience: Becoming a Responsible World Citizen.* New York: Routledge.

Cabrera, A. & Unruh, G. (2012). *Being Global: How to Think, Act, and Lead in a Transformed World.* Boston: Harvard Business School Publishing.

Rothenburg, P. (2005). *Beyond Borders: Thinking Critically About Global Issues.* London: Worth Publishers.

11
WHAT'S NEXT?

CHAPTER OVERVIEW

This chapter addresses the role of your education-abroad experience in your future life endeavors. We'll take a look at how to think about your time abroad in terms of a future career, and how you can best write and talk about that experience to a prospective employer. We end with a discussion of how you can stay connected to the host culture, even if you are planning to live permanently back home.

Reentry fiction: It's been a year now

Sam stared out of his dormitory room window, and saw the endless rows of chairs set up on the perfectly manicured green lawn. Today was graduation day. He glanced at the clock, and noted that he had three-and-a-half-hours left of being a college student. It had been a wonderful ride, with many ups and downs. But, on reflection, Sam decided the "ups" far outweighed the "downs."

His seven months in Italy had most definitely been one of those wonderful "ups," he thought, with the first couple of months back home a serious "down." But squeezing the toothpaste onto his brush, he smiled wryly as he acknowledged to himself that there had been some rough times in Italy, too—although those moments were now dim memories, or had become comfortable anecdotes that he trotted out at parties to amuse his friends.

Two weeks to relax, one week to move to Boston, and then he'd begin his new job. It was his ability to speak Italian fairly fluently that had tipped the marketing job in his favor. Angela, his new boss, had told him so when she'd called to offer him the position. With a couple of their larger clients venturing into the Italian market, the company had decided that Sam's language ability could only be an asset. To think, it had been a coin toss that decided whether he went to Italy or France.

As Sam locked his dorm-room door for what would be one of the last times, he remembered how much he'd hated being back on campus at the start of his senior year. Over the summer, after returning from Italy, he'd holed up at home in Kansas City. He didn't see much of his friends, spending most of his time composing emails or Skyping Maria and checking out her Facebook posts. He still believed his folks were secretly pleased when his long-distance romance with Maria fizzled out after a month and a half of frantic long-distance communication. It just wasn't the same as being together in Italy.

Swiping his ID in the dining hall, he recalled his minor rebellion against all American food his first semester back. He'd relented now, and often ate fast food and burgers, but the coffee—there he would remain firm. He'd learned to appreciate a good, small, but strong cup of coffee in Italy, and had found himself a couple of excellent coffee shops close to campus where he went weekly to indulge his newly acquired coffee habit. He'd also found a couple of great little Italian places to eat in town, one of them run by a lively Italian couple from Venice. So when he tired of food-service fare, he'd hike across town and enjoy a good antipasto and a heaping plate of gnocchi—and profit from the opportunity to exercise his Italian skills. Sam grimaced as he slopped a spoonful of runny yellowish scrambled eggs onto his plate.

Looking around for a familiar face in the sea of grazing students, Sam realized that he had kept the habit, developed while abroad, of taking time out to enjoy a good meal. Glancing at his tray, he thought that "good meal" might be stretching it a little when it came to what he was about to eat. A leisurely meal wasn't always possible—not with a hectic college schedule—but he'd found that he appreciated the benefits of relaxing and chatting over food, rather than using mealtimes as brief refueling stops. He saw Eiko and Jayden waving to him and went over to join them.

Sam had met Eiko last semester through a college program that paired people who wanted to practice their language skills. Unfortunately there had been no Italian student to match with Sam, but he'd been happy to meet Eiko and help her practice her English, and along the way he'd learned some basic words of Japanese from her. Over the semester, he realized that simply being able to speak to someone who'd had similar experiences to his, and who was adjusting to another people and place, made him feel more at home and helped him settle back into life on campus again. Through Eiko, he'd also met a few more international students, some of whom had become good friends, and he now had offers of free room and board in South Africa and Argentina, if he ever ventured to those parts of the world. Before going to Italy, he'd never really thought much about the international students on campus, content to hang out with his own group of American friends.

They bussed their trays and agreed to share a drink at the graduation bash that night. Jayden was freaking out about leaving college, unsure of what he wanted to do next and hating that the whole experience was coming to an end. Sam had surprised himself by how calm he felt; in fact he was rather looking forward to the next phase of his life in Boston. He'd miss his friends, as was the case when he left Italy, but he knew that he'd keep in touch with those who were really important to him, and probably lose touch with others. Change didn't seem to bother him too much anymore...

As he re-knotted his tie, checking in the bathroom mirror that it was straight, Sam felt the buzz of excitement and awe in the moment. The graduation party was in full swing, and he was having a lot more fun than he'd had at the ceremony, with the speeches and honorary-degree presentations dragging on. His time in Italy seemed far away, as, strangely, did the four college years that had just ended. But both experiences had marked him for life, and as the thumping beat of the music hit him as he walked out of the bathroom door, Sam felt content.

> **REENTERING STUDENT QUOTES**
>
> ➤ "I've gained an ability to focus and define more of my goals."
> ➤ "I've learned how my experience has changed me, and I'm still struggling to learn how to best adapt to those changes."
> ➤ "I learned a certain measure of self-discipline, and that will have an impact on my future."
> ➤ "I feel as though I am an entirely different person! I have a whole new view on the world after having experienced another culture and people."
> ➤ "I find I am much more open to people and able to talk to anyone about anything. This used to make me so anxious, and now I actually enjoy doing it. I am more engaged with my current city, current friends, and current self."
> ➤ "I became a more logic-oriented person... I got into graduate school... I got really good at Excel, and that helped me become more comfortable with computer programming, which is probably going to be a huge part of my career in the future, so that's good."
> ➤ "I feel more relaxed (e.g. not rushing through dinner—taking like two hours to sit and eat and talk and enjoy company), and I'm also venturing out and doing new things on my own."

And now?

You wanted to go abroad, you applied, you got accepted, you went, you studied, you learned, and you came back. Now you're trying to figure out what all that means for you today—and tomorrow. You know that your intercultural experience brought changes in your interests, beliefs, and assumptions. But what might you do with those new qualities? What will these changes mean for your future studies and career? As Eleanor Roosevelt[1] once wrote, "When you are genuinely interested in one thing, it will always lead to something else." Your passion for learning abroad, for exploring cultures, languages, the world, will have an impact on where you go from here. What exactly that looks like, you don't yet know.

It may be difficult at first to know exactly how you've changed, and even harder to predict how those changes will affect you in the future. But in reentry, you can and should begin to think productively about these questions, and consider the ways in which you've advanced since you left on your intercultural journey.

Below is a list of changes often cited by recent returnees. Do any ring true for you? What others would you add to the list?

- I have more confidence now.
- I expect more of myself.
- I feel a clearer sense of identity.
- I am more realistic about myself.
- I better appreciate what I have.
- I feel more independent.
- I am better able to see other points of view.
- I am more apt to think about how others' experiences differ from my own.
- I am better able to help others see the value in cultural diversity.
- I am better at teaching, explaining, or guiding.
- I am more patient.
- I am more dedicated to my work.

Making your intercultural experience work for you

As we saw in Chapter 10, international experience is increasingly seen as a key asset in corporations and other organizations worldwide. No matter what field you are interested in pursuing, don't be shy about marketing your international and intercultural skills! Even if you plan to enter a field that has little to do with international issues, your experience abroad can enhance your application.

But your experience abroad won't speak for you. As career expert Cheryl Matherly writes:

> It is simply not enough to seek an international experience—the experience itself has little value for an employer. The savvy job seeker must be able to speak about this experience in terms of the transferable skills that he or she developed while abroad and how they can be applied to the workplace. For many students, this can be an enormous challenge.[2]

Take some time to think carefully about how you want to talk about your international experience on your resume or in job interviews. Be specific so that the person you're talking to understands the impact of that experience. In addition to the more obvious skills, such as foreign language translation and specific country knowledge, think about the following skills you probably gained as a result of your intercultural experience:

- **Negotiation:** Finding ways to get what you need even when the system is confusing or different from what you're used to

- **Adapting to change:** Feeling comfortable with the initial shock of a new environment; having confidence in your ability to ride through the change
- **Comfort with diversity:** Being able to work well with different kinds of people; making the most of different people's approaches to the same task
- **Flexibility:** Knowing you can operate well in different environments and under different rules
- **Learning:** Being able to learn independently; having confidence in your ability to learn quickly
- **Broadened scope:** Knowing that there are always multiple ways to approach a problem or issue
- **Independence:** Having the wherewithal to figure out what needs to be done, even when you're not familiar with the territory, and making it happen
- **Confidence:** Becoming comfortable with finding your way in new situations, and not letting fear of the unknown get in the way of accomplishing a goal
- **Creative problem-solving:** Approaching problems with an open mind, and discovering novel ways to arrive at solutions
- **Comfort with ambiguity:** Learning to "go with the flow" and proceed even when you aren't quite sure of the rules or parameters in a situation

Take a moment to identify and jot down a few other newly developed or enhanced skills that apply to you.

If you are applying for a job or volunteer position, think about these skills—and others you may have gained—and jot down specific examples that illustrate each one. Offering specifics (while keeping anecdotes brief and professional) will help a potential employer understand how those skills might play out concretely in a work or volunteer situation. As you think about which skills to highlight, be sure you are taking into consideration the requirements of the position you are interested in. Identify the key skills called for in the job description, and then consider how you can link skills you developed through your experience abroad to these. For example, does the job description call for excellent communication skills? Think about the experience you gained in communicating effectively through cultural and language differences. Does it call for the ability to build relationships with various stakeholders? Think about your experience developing relationships with people very different from you, and how you found points of commonality. Tell those stories—again, briefly—to help your prospective employer understand how, exactly, you went about achieving those goals.

Let's take an example. Suppose you are in a job interview, and the interviewer asks you, "Tell me about an experience you've had where you worked collaboratively with a diverse team—one where people came with different experiences and skills—to achieve a goal."

How would you answer, drawing on your experience abroad? Let's look at a not-so-good answer, and then a better one:

A weak answer

> When I was studying abroad in Argentina, I had to do a group project with four other international students. We had to interview somebody who worked in the media and give a class presentation on it. Their Spanish was not as good as mine, so I worked up the interview questions and ran the interview, and they transcribed it and organized the information for the presentation. For the presentation, we decided that I should be the main presenter, and the others added in some information about the company that our interviewee worked for.

Why is this a weak answer? Here you're really not talking about working collaboratively; rather, this is an example of one person taking charge—which is not what the employer's question asked you to talk about.

A better answer

> When I was studying abroad in Argentina, I was part of a four-person group doing a project on national media for a media studies class. The group members were all international students, from four different countries. Our first step was to figure out what each of our strengths were, and how we could put those to use in the project. One person was really skilled at design, so she did the layout and slides, and another was a good writer, so he did the write-ups with input from everyone. I had strong oral language skills, so I did the interviews. We all worked together to come up with interview questions and decide how the final product would come together. It was great learning from other people's experience and seeing how the final product was so much better than what any one of us could have done alone. And doing that all in another language meant that we sometimes did not fully understand each other's meaning, so we had to stay patient, ask lots of questions, and trust that in the end we'd find a common understanding. It was sometimes challenging, but it was rewarding to be able to make it all come together.

This answer highlights the collaborative nature of the experience—which is what the employer is looking for—and demonstrates that you were able to effectively work across difference and to see the value in that.

According to broad employer surveys in the US, UK, and Canada,[3] among the top skills employers value today are

- Organization and time management
- Ability to work effectively with customers or clients
- Ability to work effectively in a team
- People skills and managing emotions at work

- Written and oral communication skills
- Problem-solving skills

These are all skills that an education-abroad experience can help you develop. Before you send out your CV/resume or go on a job interview, it's worth taking some time to think through how your experience abroad has helped you become more skilled in each of these areas. Take that to a more concrete level, too, by thinking about the kinds of questions a prospective employer might ask you, and how you can use your education-abroad experience to demonstrate your abilities.

You can start with the following list; find more in your university's career office, or online.

- What experiences have you had during college that have prepared you for this job?
- How do you handle situations where there are no clear-cut rules? Can you give us an example?
- What role do you tend to play when you are working in a team? What's an example of that?
- What are one or two experiences you've had in college that allowed you to learn in ways you didn't expect?
- How do you handle tasks when you are under pressure? Can you give us an example?
- How would you describe your communication style? Tell us about a time when you had to adapt to a different communication style in order to get a task completed.
- What are some mistakes you have made that have taught you important lessons?
- Tell us about a time when you've worked with somebody who had a different perspective from your own on the task at hand. How did you manage that situation?
- When you are part of a team, how do you help ensure that everybody gets to contribute their best work? Give us an example.
- Tell us about a time you took a risk in a project or some task. How did it play out, and what did you learn?
- What is one accomplishment over the past four years that you're especially proud of?

Your written materials: CV/resume and cover letter

Your CV or resume and cover letter are your way to get a foot in the door: They are the first impression you'll make on an employer, and they're what the employer will use to determine whether or not to invite you in for an interview. There is plenty of good advice available on writing effective materials in your university's career center/careers service, and in dozens of books on the topic—so we won't go into a lot of detail here. In terms of your experience abroad, we recommend that you include it on your resume/CV, and that you mention it in your cover letter in a way that links the experience to the job you are seeking. For example, imagine Erin is applying for a job in public relations with a healthcare organization. She might include the following in her cover letter:

> During the semester I spent studying in Japan, I faced the challenge of communicating effectively with people who often held very different assumptions about the world from my own. This experience taught me the real-life lesson that I had previously only learned in the abstract: that taking time to understand people's frames of reference will help enormously in communicating your messages to them.

You can consider what you might say in your own context, given your particular experience abroad and the kinds of roles you are interested in. There are many ways to approach this, but you should be sure to make a clear connection between what you learned abroad and the skills required for the role.

What does the research say?

In reviewing the literature, intercultural scholar Mitchell Hammer and colleagues[4] remind us that intercultural competence is generally characterized by qualities such as comfort with ambiguity, open-mindedness, empathy, ability to handle stress, and interpersonal skills. While you are not guaranteed to have developed these skills just because you've spent time on an education-abroad program, returnees are, broadly speaking, pretty likely to have further developed one or more of them. And these are the very characteristics that make young job-seekers attractive to many organizations.

In fact, there is research bearing this out. Researchers Philip Gardner, Inge Steglitz and Linda Gross[5] ran focus groups with business professionals and found that they identified employees with international experience as having higher abilities in the following important workplace competencies:

- Working independently
- Taking on new kinds of tasks
- Using knowledge in new settings
- Coming up with novel solutions to problems
- Interacting well with coworkers
- Getting along well with people different from you
- Being sensitive to cultural differences at work
- Becoming comfortable with new situations
- Learning from experience

This list gives you the language to translate some of the value of your experience abroad into specific skills that potential employers may value. You may not feel that every item on the lists applies to you, but think about which ones do, and how you can describe the role of your experience abroad in helping you develop them.

Your time abroad may also have simply given you more clarity about your career goals. A number of researchers[6] have found that experiences abroad helped students focus their career aspirations. Researchers Emily Morris and Joan Gillespie,[7] in a survey of several thousand former education-abroad participants, found that about half of people in non-globally focused jobs, and about three-quarters of those in globally focused jobs, felt that their experience abroad had made a difference in their careers. Another study,[8] involving about 200 US business students, had similar results, with about two-thirds reporting that education abroad had made a difference in their career paths. (It's important to note that these are individuals' own impressions of the impact of the experience abroad, not an objective measure.) Even if you do not feel at the moment that your experience abroad has affected your career plans, you may—with hindsight—see a connection down the road. It's often difficult to understand the impact that an experience is having on us while we're still having it!

There is also a good deal of research demonstrating the value that employers place on skills gained during education abroad. In a survey of several hundred US employers, researchers from the Council for International Educational Exchange and Penn State University[9] found that human resources managers—those often responsible for hiring entry-level employees—placed relatively high value on education-abroad experience. However, they also found that while employers in general value the skills related to international experience—such as flexibility and adapting to new situations—they did not always connect those skills to education abroad. This means, as we saw earlier, that it's important to reflect ahead of time so that you can clearly explain the connections between your experience abroad and your marketable skills.

Beyond career: Staying connected

Your career is one of the most important long-term outcomes of your time abroad, but we don't want to overlook the value of all of the personal development—and, simply, the enjoyment—that people experience while learning abroad. Once you're back home, it's easy to feel disconnected from the host culture, and this can detract from the benefits you've gained. But there are things you can do to stay connected. For instance, you can take advantage of films, food, literature, newspapers and magazines, and language conversation groups. You can join online groups and language exchanges, use apps to keep up your language skills, listen to podcasts in the target language. You can give your time to be a "buddy" to an international student on campus, you can host a foreign visitor through an international business group in the community, attend international events at your college or university. You can volunteer to help with activities for international students on campus, like new student orientation, or for organizations in the community. You can become active in civic or business organizations that deal with intercultural issues, volunteer to speak to classes or groups on your host country or your intercultural experience, visit primary schools to talk to children about your host country. Opportunities abound.

Becoming an intercultural leader

A final word on using your experience abroad to make a difference. As a result of your education-abroad experience, whether you fully realize it or not, you have gained a deeper understanding of intercultural relationships. We hope that this book has helped you begin to see the various ways in which that is true. You may have greater insight into how culture shapes values. You may feel more empathy toward people with values different from yours. You may have come to appreciate beliefs and traditions very different from your own. You may spend more time thinking about the challenges others face in their lives based on who they are and where they live. Because you have developed in all these ways, you are now better situated to help others begin to see and understand those differences, too.

In today's world, there is a great need for more people to play that role. Consider how you can contribute, even in small ways, to helping others begin to see across the gulfs and barriers that divide us. Speak up when you hear somebody disparage another culture out of ignorance or fear. Speak out when you have an opportunity to share your intercultural point of view—in class, in meetings, in letters to the editor or to your elected officials. Help friends and family who haven't had the opportunity to cross cultural lines learn more about others who are different from them, by making introductions, by sharing news, movies, stories. In these ways you can be, and most likely already are, a leader in your community, helping to bridge cultural gaps, reduce distrust, and create greater understanding across cultural groups.

It's been a year now: Considering Sam's experience

Back to our story of Sam, returning home from Italy. Sam seems to be in a really good place and most likely would be considered at the end of his reentry transition. He is graduating from college and has a job in another city, Boston. He got his job in part because his experience abroad helped him improve his Italian skills, and those language skills gave him the edge over other candidates. He seems to have been able to carry on some of the behaviors and values he adapted to while in Italy. For example, he enjoys a leisurely meal where both the food and the conversation with his meal companions are important. However, he seems aware that American culture is more fast-paced than Italian culture, so has learned that he has to carve out time for this slower pace of life, and realistically cannot achieve it all the time.

In Eiko, Sam found a new friend, a person who can appreciate his experiences, as she is an international student who is herself in the midst of her own time abroad. Once again, he was realistic in his expectations. When he could not find an Italian conversation partner at his school, he selected someone from another culture to partner up with, and still found pleasure in that relationship.

Sam seems to have realized the just like coming home from Italy, leaving college and moving to Boston will be another transition. But, having successfully gone through reentry, he is now more confident, less nervous, and more accepting of change. He knows that he will miss his friends and the familiar places of his college town, but at the same time realizes he will make new friends, stay in touch with the old friends whose relationships can be renegotiated as circumstances dictate, and will get to find new places in Boston to grow fond of.

Remember, Sam's reentry was *not* without turbulence. He broke up with his girlfriend and spent much of the first few months back home moping in his Kansas City bedroom at his parents' house. But by working proactively through reentry, Sam has managed the challenges and realized the benefits that education abroad offered him.

Notes

1 Roosevelt, E. (1960). *You Learn by Living: Eleven Keys for a More Fulfilling Life.* New York: HarperCollins. Quote p. 14.
2 Matherly, C. (2005). Effective marketing of international experiences to employers. In M. Tillman (Ed.), *Impact of Education Abroad on Career Development, Vol. 1* (pp. 9–10). Stamford, CT: American Institute for Foreign Study. Accessed December 3, 2017 at: www.aifsabroad.com/advisors/pdf/Impact_of_Education_AbroadI.pdf. Quote p. 9.
3 National Association of College and Employers. (2018). *Job Outlook 2018.* Bethlehem, PA: NACE; UK Commission for Employment and Skills. (2016). *Employer Skills Survey 2015.* London: UKCES; Aon Hewitt. (2016). *Developing Canada's Future Workforce: A Survey of Large Private-sector Employers.* Toronto: Aon Hewitt.
4 Hammer, M.R., Nishida, H., & Wiseman, R.L. (1996). The influence of situational prototypes on dimensions of intercultural communication competence. *Journal of Cross-Cultural Psychology, 27*(3), 267–282.
5 Gardener, P. Steglitz, I., & Gross, L. (2009). Translating study abroad experiences for workplace competencies. *Peer Review, 11*(4), 19–22.
6 Hannigan, T.P. (2001). The effects of work abroad experiences on career development of U.S. undergraduates. *Frontiers: The Interdisciplinary Journal of Study Abroad, 7,* 1–23; Paige, R.M., Fry, G.W., Stallman, E.M., Josic, J., & Jon, J. (2009). Study abroad for global engagement: The long-term impact of mobility experiences. *Intercultural Education, 20*(S1–2), S29–44.
7 Norris, E.M. & Gillespie, J. (2009). How study abroad shapes global careers: Evidence from the United States. *Journal of Studies in International Education, 13*(3), 382–397.
8 Orahood, T., Kruze, L., & Pearson, E. (2004). The impact of study abroad on business students' career goals. *The Interdisciplinary Journal of Study Abroad, 10,* 117–130.
9 Trooboff, S., Berg, M.V., & Rayman, J. (2007). Employer attitudes toward study abroad. *Frontiers: The Interdisciplinary Journal of Study Abroad, 15,* 17–33.

FOOD FOR THOUGHT

1. What might an employer not understand about your intercultural experience that you can help clarify? Why is it important?
2. What preconceptions might an employer have about education abroad, or about you as a former participant? Why might they hold those preconceptions?
3. What are the skills you began to develop while abroad that you feel are "unfinished"? How can you continue to develop them?
4. Is intercultural understanding something a person can gain second-hand? In other words, does it take direct contact with another culture? Why or why not? Is it possible to help others become more interculturally oriented if they haven't had that kind of contact?

Suggestions for further reading

Bashan, L. (2017). *Global: An Extraordinary Guide for Ordinary Heroes*. Dorset, UK: Red Press.

Bolles, R. (2018) *What Color Is Your Parachute? A Practical Manual for Job-hunters and Career Changers*. New York: Ten Speed Press.

Mueller, S.L. and Overmann, M. (2014). *Working World: Careers in International Education, Exchange, and Development*. Washington, DC: Georgetown University Press.

Pollack, L. (2012). *Getting from College to Career: Your Essential Guide to Surviving in the Real World*. New York: HarperBusiness.

Roadtrip Nation (2015). *Roadmap: The Get-it-together Guide for Figuring Out What to Do with Your Life*. San Francisco: Chronicle Books.

CONCLUSION

At the beginning of this book, we suggested that you take from it what is most useful for you, and we hope that you have done this. We also suggested that by the end of the book, both the challenges and opportunities reentry offers you would be clear to you, and we hope that they are. In the introduction we also defined intercultural reentry for you. In case you can't recall what we said, here is our definition for you again: reentry is the process of adjusting to life at home, after a significant intercultural experience in a host culture different from the home culture. Reentry includes the process of reflecting on and making sense of those intercultural interactions, and of incorporating those experiences into your life back home, your understanding of yourself, and what you envision for your future.

A process takes place over time (as you've learned, that time can be long or short—it depends on the student). The education-abroad experience is a significant, impactful intercultural experience for most students, and you've learned the myriad ways in which it can be seen as such. Points of difference between your home and host cultures often come into sharper relief upon reentry, and you've learned how to explore and explain those differences, both for yourself and for those around you. You've seen the importance of the process of reflecting, with some specificity, and in a structured way, on your experiences abroad and in reentry. We hope you'll continue to reflect! You've also learned multiple ways to figure out new skills, knowledge, values, ways of being and seeing in reentry that can be incorporated into your life at the personal, academic, and professional levels.

Remember that your reentry experience after studying abroad is unique and is your own to do with what you will. No matter the context of your experience abroad, different individuals set out different goals and have different hopes and expectations for their time learning abroad, and the realization (or not) of those goals, hopes, and expectations depends on a whole host of factors: your individual personality, the local environment, the degree and types of differences between your home culture and the new one, and so on. Recognize that your experience abroad cannot be reduced to a rational set of logical choices, that your feelings will have played a significant role in what you chose to do at every turn throughout your sojourn, and that those in turn will have an impact in reentry.

Remember also that you will experience intercultural reentry every time you come home after any significant sojourn in a host culture, and that each reentry experience will be different. If you are lucky enough to have many more intercultural experiences in your life as you grow older and establish yourself in a career, spending significant amounts of time away from what you consider your home culture, you may come to a point where you consider home to be in multiple places, to be in more than one culture, and to include different sets of people. And that is OK. In fact, we would suggest that is more than OK, that it is healthy and demonstrates an ability to integrate different worldviews, use multiple intercultural communication skills, and adapt to different environments effectively.

If you remember nothing else from what you have read in this book six months from now (and of course we do hope you remember and apply a lot more!), remember that reentry is normal, it is a transition, there are both shared experiences with other returnees and experiences that are just yours, that reentry is experienced with differing intensities for different students, and that there are both positives and negatives to this transition.

In Zimbabwe, when someone goes on a journey, people say in English "Go well," in Shona they say "Fambai zvakanaka," and in Nedebele they say "Hamba kahle." Now, at the end of this book, we wish you the best on your journey through intercultural reentry and are convinced you will emerge on the other side all the better for your experiences. Good luck!

RESOURCES

Now that you have read and worked through our book, we want to provide you with some additional resources that you may find useful as you successfully manage your intercultural reentry.

First, we'd recommend that you seek out resources available to you at your university. If you're not sure what's available on your campus to you as a returnee, your best bet may be to start with an inquiry to the study-abroad or education-abroad office, an international student office or center, or an international student group. Even if they don't have specific intercultural reentry resources available, or interesting opportunities for you, they can very likely help point you in the right direction.

Second, below we provide some resources available to you online that we think you will find useful. We've divided these resources into different categories to help you most easily find the kind of resource you may be looking for:

Understanding cultural differences resources

CARLA (Center for Advanced Research in Language Learning)
University of Minnesota
http://carla.umn.edu/index.html

Browse the CARLA website for information and leads on other resources that may be of use to you in reentry.

Geert Hofstede
http://geerthofstede.com/training-consulting/online-lectures/

Watch videos describing six different dimensions of cultural variation as explained by Hofstede.

Hofstede Insights
www.hofstede-insights.com/product/compare-countries/

This resource allows you to compare different countries' positions on various dimensions of cultural variation.

Mitchell Hammer
The Intercultural Development Inventory.
https://idiinventory.com/wp-content/uploads/2017/01/HAMMER-IDI-STUDY-ABROAD-ARTICLE-2012.pdf

Read this article available as a pdf at the link above to learn more about intercultural competence.

Reentry specific resources

The Africa Report
Repats: Ten stories of African Diaspora who returned home.
www.theafricareport.com/North-Africa/repats-ten-stories-of-african-diaspora-who-retunred-home.html

This resource, while not specifically about students, still offers a really interesting set of observations and descriptions of Africans returning home to their country of origin after being away, providing multiple insights into reentry.

Alex Bergen
Reverse culture shock – The first 24 hours.
www.youtube.com/watch?v=lHN0tVd9G8I

This resource is a vlog personal testimony of an American sojourner's first 24 hours home in the US after two years in Denmark.

Carleton College
Transitioning back to the United States and Carleton.
https://apps.carleton.edu/curricular/ocs/planning/transition/

Hear from students about their transitions between different cultures in this video.

Frances Carruthers
My reverse culture shock: Returning from a year abroad is tough.
www.theguardian.com/education/2017/jul/20/reverse-culture-shock-tough-adjusting-home-studying-abroad

This article from *The Guardian* is written by a student who spent a year in Canada and then went back to the UK.

James Citron and Vija Mendelson
Coming home: Relationships, roots, and unpacking
www.fitchburgstate.edu/uploads/files/InternationalEducation/Coming
 HomeArticle.PDF

Read this short article that has a great comparison of experiences of a good and bad day in reentry.

Danielle Desimone
Reverse culture shock: Expectation vs. reality.
www.goabroad.com/articles/study-abroad/reverse-culture-shock-
 expectation-vs-reality

This short article does a nice job of discussing reentry expectations versus the reality of reentry for some returnees.

Homecoming Revolution
Reasons to return to South Africa.
http://homecomingrevolution.com/south-africa/

Take a quick look at the list of reasons this organization suggests for why people who have left South Africa return—the specifics of what people might love in reentry are interesting and fun.

Miyako
Reverse culture shock.
www.youtube.com/watch?v=XjgRUdzGkqE

This resource is another vlog personal testimony of a student returnee coming home to the US from America.

University of the Pacific
What's up with culture?
www2.pacific.edu/sis/culture/

We suggest you focus on Module Two, "Welcome Back! Now What?"

Georgetown University
Re-entry resources: What is reverse culture shock?
https://studyabroad.georgetown.edu/alumni-re-entry#

Take a look at this slideshow from Georgetown's counseling service on the experience of reverse culture shock.

USA Today College

7 ways to cope with reentry shock after studying abroad.
http://college.usatoday.com/2016/06/05/7-ways-to-cope-with-re-entry-shock-after-studying-abroad/

This is a good, concise article from USA Today on the reentry experience.

Global perspective resources

SIETAR USA (Society for Intercultural Training, Education and Research)
www.sietarusa.org/
SIETAR Europa
www.sietareu.org/

These two websites might provide you with useful information and ideas for effective integration of your experiences into a more globally focused perspective.

Christina Ferrari Janis Fine
Developing global perspectives in short-term study abroad: High-impact learning through curriculum, co-curriculum and community.
https://digitalcommons.kennesaw.edu/cgi/viewcontent.cgi?referer=https://www.google.com/&httpsredir=1&article=1189&context=jgi

Read this academic article with an interesting focus on the development of global perspectives.

Reflection

Trent University
How do I… write a reflection?
www.trentu.ca/academicskills/documents/Reflectivewriting.pdf

Read this short article on reflective writing from this Canadian university.

University of New South Wales
Reflective writing.
https://student.unsw.edu.au/reflective-writing

Browse this Australian university's web pages on reflective writing for students to help you with your reflection in reentry.

Career, resume, and letter writing resources

University of Minnesota Learning Abroad
Re-entry handbook.

> https://umabroad.umn.edu/assets/files/PDFs/Career%20Integration/Re-Entry%20Handbook%202013.pdf

This is an excellent discussion of reentry from the University of Minnesota, with an emphasis on career planning.

> *Liz Ryan*
> Smart job seekers break these ten resume-writing rules.
> www.forbes.com/sites/lizryan/2017/05/19/smart-job-seekers-break-these-ten-resume-writing-rules/#761088095e81

Watch this short video on Forbes.com suggesting ways to improve your resume.

> *Monster.com*
> How to write a resume: Resume tips.
> www.monster.com/career-advice/article/how-to-write-a-resume

Read the tips for writing an effective resume; remember to include the knowledge and skills your education abroad and reentry have helped you learn and develop.

> *Purdue Online Writing Lab* **(OWL)**
> Job skills checklist.
> https://owl.english.purdue.edu/owl/resource/626/1/
> What is an action verb?
> https://owl.english.purdue.edu/owl/resource/543/1/
> Categorized list of action verbs.
> https://owl.english.purdue.edu/owl/resource/543/02/
> Example employment documents.
> https://owl.english.purdue.edu/owl/resource/734/1/

Use these resources from OWL to be specific in your descriptions of skills and knowledge gained through your education-abroad and reentry experiences when writing resumes, letters of application, or preparing for interviews.

Remember, you need to take some time to find the kind of reentry resources and opportunities that are most beneficial to you, but they *are* out there. You just need to put some initiative into seeking out the ones that are right for you. We hope the list we provided above gives you a good start in the process.

INDEX

abstract conceptualization 31
Adler, N.J. 39–43
age 19–20
ambiguity: comfort with 30, 87, 89, 120, 123
assumptions 19–20, 33, 49–50, 102, 112
Australia 21, 41, 79

Basseches, M. 48
Bennett, M.J. 90–91, 94
Bridges, W. 47–49
Brown, L. 32, 52, 92, 104

Canada 21, 96–97, 104–105, 121
career 89–93, 111–112, 119–124
China 45, 53, 104, 108
Christofi, V. 12, 41, 104
collectivism 22, 100–101
communication 58, 62, 80; and campus 63; and high context vs. low context 100–101; and positive & negative 65
comparisons 85, 99
concrete experience 31
connections: maintaining 77–78, 124–125
Costa Rica 23
country of origin 20–21, 24; and threats 24
cultural distance 22–23
Cyprus 12, 41–42

detached style 40
dimensions of cultural variation 99–103
Doyle, D. 61, 64

Ecclestone, K. 50–51
elevator speech 59–61
emotions 7, 19, 23, 122
empathy 23, 52, 114, 123, 125
employment *see* career
England 12, 16–17, 23–24, 41, 56–57, 65
ethnography 33
experiential learning 31
extraversion 29

Facebook 33, 68, 117
Fine, J.B. 23
friendship 70–79; and styles 75

Gardner, P. 89, 123
Gaw, K. 93
gender 17, 19–20, 94, 112
global citizenship 109, 114
global citizenship model 109; and civic engagement 109; and competence 109; and mindset 109
Goldstein, S.B. 24
Greece 20, 41

Hall, E.T. 100–101
Hammer, M. 123
high power distance 102–103
Hofstede, G. 101, 102
home 7–9; and differences between home and host culture 21; and readiness to return 21

identity 24, 40, 42, 51–52, 58, 73, 103
individualism 100–101

Ingram, R. 47
intellectual capital 111–112
intercultural understanding: model of 90–91
introversion 29
Ireland 23

Japan 20, 42, 52, 64, 70, 79, 123
Jarvis, P. 50
Javidan, M. 111

Kartoshkina 64, 104
Kauffmann 93
Kenya 71, 96–97, 104–105
Kim, Y.Y. 58
Kolb, A.Y. 31–32
Kolb model 31–32

LaBrack, B. 42–43
language: and challenges 64; and skills 23–24
low power distance 102–103

Matherly, C. 119
McCabe, J. 75
Mendelson, V. 43
Merriam, S. 33
Mezirow J. 50
models of transformational learning 50
Morais, D. 109

New Zealand 51, 65, 104
Netherlands 83–84, 94
Nguyen, A. 23
Northern Ireland 12

observer perspective 10–11

Perry, W. 86–87
Perry model 86
Pritchard, R. 12
psychological capital 111–112
Pusch, M.D. 40–41, 43

race 20
reentry styles *see* returnee styles
reflection 33; and relationship 71–72; and self 85

reflective: observation 31; thinking 87–88
renegotiation 58; and identity 58
returnee styles: alienated 39; alienator 40; bumpie 42; detached 40; free spirited 40; integrator 40; proactive 39; reassimilator 40; rebellious 40; resocialized 39; resocializer 40; smoothie 42; transformer 40
Roberts, C. 32–33
romance 76–77

Sicola, L. 64
situational variables 22
Smith, S. 58
social capital 111–112
social media 70–71, 77
social responsibility 109
Sri Lanka 12
Stephenson-Abetz, J. 47
stereotype threats 24
Streitwieser, B. 113
Sussman, N.M. 42, 52
Szkudlarek, B. 22, 92

Taiwan 12, 68
Thailand 23
Thompson, C. 12, 41, 104
time: length studied abroad 23; monochronic time orientation 101; polychronic time orientation 101
Ting Toomey, S. 40
transition stages 47–48
transitions 47–51

UK 12, 17, 21, 27, 52, 79, 92, 104
unpacking 89
US 21, 24, 72

Vietnam 23, 104

Williams, T.R. 33, 92

Yang, M. 92
Yoshida, T. 42, 64

Zimbabwe 5–6, 10–11, 13, 41, 64, 129